SUPERGOLF

Also by John Andrisani

Natural Golf

101 Supershots

Grip It and Rip It

The Wedge-Game Pocket Companion

SuperGolf

Setup, Swing and Shotmaking Secrets From the Best of the PGA Hall of Fame

RICK GRAYSON *and*
JOHN ANDRISANI

HarperCollins*Publishers*

HarperCollins books may be purchased for educational, business, or sales promotional use. For information, please write to: Special Markets Department, HarperCollins Publishers Inc., 10 East 53rd Street, New York, New York 10022.

FIRST EDITION

Designed by Irving Perkins Associates

Library of Congress Cataloging-in-Publication Data

Andrisani, John.
   Supergolf: setup, swing, and shotmaking secrets from the best of the PGA Hall of
Fame / John Andrisani and Rick Grayson. — 1st ed.
     p. cm.
   ISBN 0-06-270157-6
   1. Golf. 2. Swing (Golf). 3. Golf—Drive. 4. Golfers—Biography.
I. Grayson, Rick, 1954–   . II. Title.
GV965.A57   1996
796.352'3—dc20   96-9739

96 97 98 99 00 ❖/RRD 10 9 8 7 6 5 4 3 2 1

CONTENTS

5. Woodwork

6. Long Way "Home"

7. The Iron Man

8. Houdini Is Alive

9. Sand Savvy

FOREWORD

This is a book about great players and their phenomenal setup, swing and shotmaking methods. Some of these players are in the World Golf Hall of Fame. Others look destined to be honored there one day.

I suppose the idea for writing this book, at least on a subconscious level, came to me over twenty years ago. In 1974, I traveled to Pinehurst Country Club with a golfing friend. That year, President Gerald Ford came to North Carolina to dedicate the new World Golf Hall of Fame. Ben Hogan, Byron Nelson, Gary Player, Arnold Palmer and Jack Nicklaus were among the inductees present for the ceremony. It was satisfying to know that these living legends were being immortalized in the same way that Babe Ruth, Joe DiMaggio and Jackie Robinson had been honored in Cooperstown, New York.

My idea surfaced again approximately two years ago, when I heard the World Golf Hall of Fame was going to be moved to Florida and become part of the new World Golf Village, to be located about eight miles north of St. Augustine and twenty-two miles south of downtown Jacksonville. At first, I felt kind of nostalgic for Pinehurst. However, when I found out about the big plans for the new Hall, I was happy to hear it was being relocated in a bigger and better home. Scheduled to open in 1998, it is to be a 75,000-square-foot state-of-the-art structure. The village site itself will include a resort hotel and conference center, golf library, championship golf course and golf academy.

I felt even more compelled to write this book when I thought of all the many new golfers looking to get off on the right foot, and the millions of veterans who truly can't hit the broad side of a barn. What better way to help newcomers to the game get off to a good start, or help golfers improve their games, than to reveal to them the unique techniques of the world's greatest professionals.

I ran the idea past Patricia Leasure, the executive editor of HarperCollins Publishers, explaining to her that the book would also tell readers how these superstars got into golf and about the great shots they hit in tournaments. A new golfer herself, she was very excited about learning some golf history and new shotmaking techniques. So HarperCollins agreed to publish *SuperGolf*.

It's important to note that, in addition to the Hall of Famers included in this book, there are "Future Famer" golfing greats, whom co-author Rick Grayson and I believe are on track to enter the hallowed Hall. Time will tell, of course.

I first met Grayson through the articles he had written for *GOLF Magazine*, where I work as senior editor of instruction. He is a Missouri-based golf instructor who is on *GOLF*'s Top 100 Best Teachers list. He has a great passion for the game of golf. No less important, he has a special eye for analyzing swings. Plus, he has conducted golf clinics with big name pros, including Payne Stewart, who is one of the Future Famers included in *SuperGolf*. He knows his stuff.

In the course of my job, I've had the opportunity to work with many of these Hall of Famers. In fact, I've written instruction books with two of them: Seve Ballesteros and Chi Chi Rodriguez. I also collaborated with Future Famers Fred Couples and John Daly.

I brought Grayson aboard because something told me we would make a good team. I was right. The book is helped greatly by the wonderful photographs, taken by Leonard Kamsler, of such fine swingers as Sam Snead and Mickey Wright. Ken Lewis' artwork adds flavor to the book and helps convey the instructional messages.

The team hopes you enjoy reading *SuperGolf* and learn a lot about how to play this great game to a higher standard. There's instruction on how to line up square, how to hit the ball powerfully, how to save shots on and around the green, how to play from trouble and more. So we don't think you can miss.

Good luck.

JOHN ANDRISANI

1

MR. METICULOUS

Jack Nicklaus is the all-time master of pre-tournament, pre-round, pre-shot preparation.

*Ever since his early days
on the PGA Tour,
Jack Nicklaus has had the
confident—some call it cocky—
look of a champion.*

Without question, Jack Nicklaus is the best golfer that ever walked planet earth. That is the consensus of golf experts, the press and galleries all over the world. There have been other names that some think are deserving of this high honor, most notably Ben Hogan and Bobby Jones. But Nicklaus possesses the sharpest golfing mind, and strategically, he's the smartest. In fact, when it comes to preparing for a tournament, he's as thorough as General Patton was in preparing for war.

Jack William Nicklaus was born on January 21, 1940, in Columbus, Ohio. As a youngster Jack played all kinds of sports. But baseball, football and basketball were three he played particularly well. He didn't take up golf seriously until the age of ten, when his father, Charles, took him over to Scioto Country Club. Jack's dad was a member there, so he felt good about putting his son in the able hands of teaching pro Jack Grout. That was the best hand-off of all time, because it turned out to be the ideal teacher-pupil relationship.

From the get-go, Grout encouraged Nicklaus to hit the ball hard. Jack, like all kids, liked that. According to Nicklaus, Grout believed that a golfer who learns to swing hard initially can usually acquire accuracy later, whereas a golfer who gets too accuracy conscious at the outset will rarely be able to make himself hit the ball hard later on. Although Grout encouraged Jack to swing with abandon, he did want Jack to keep his head steady. In fact, Grout grabbed Jack's hair, so that if he moved his head too much, he'd feel pain. Grout also tightened the reins when teaching Jack the address or setup position and the vital elements of grip, stance, aim and alignment. Sometimes these positions felt uncomfortable to Jack, but being a good student and a trusting person, he heeded Grout's advice. There's no question that he became a better player for it.

Two years after beginning golf, he broke 80. At age 13, he broke 70. At age 16, he won his state open title. At age 19, he won the

U.S. Amateur. At 21, he won the NCAA. At 22, he won the U.S. Open, beating golf's most popular player, Arnold Palmer. This victory didn't go over so well at first. Arnie's Army didn't like Nicklaus, whom they perceived as a cold, calculating big brute who had beaten their Arnie. In time, Nicklaus loosened up, lost weight and said goodbye to his crewcut. Many golf fans started to accept the fact that, in sports, a changing of the guard is an inevitable happening. They began to root for Nicklaus. The rest, as they say, is history.

During his heyday, Nicklaus combined superb shotmaking skills with unmatchable course management "smarts." Those management skills went far beyond deciding whether to hit a fade or a draw on a particular hole. They weren't just about picking the proper club either. They were about *preparing totally* for a shot.

Nicklaus' shotmaking planning processes started before he even got to the ball. In fact, they started before he got to the course. He played the round in his head the night before. By the time he arrived at the site, he pretty much knew every single shot he was going to hit that particular day. And when he was on, the round he physically played virtually matched the one he had played mentally. Nicklaus prepared so well, he never gave a shot away. He always used to say that he "never missed a shot in his head before he played it." With that kind of preparation and positive mental attitude, Nicklaus was a step ahead of his opponents before he teed off.

The fact that Nicklaus won the 1986 Masters at the age of 46, against young and talented "flat bellies" who hit the ball off the earth and putted like God, proves that there is a special quality about him. Nicklaus has a "fifteenth club" in his bag that allows him to play more efficiently than anyone else, to never give the game away. Golf aficionados will admit that they've never seen Nicklaus play a driver on a short, extremely narrow par-four hole, try to reach a par five in two by hitting a giant hook shot over a lake or charge a 50-foot putt. He's just too darn smart to make any of these stupid mistakes.

That's why he was voted *Player of the Century* by *GOLF Magazine* in 1988. That's why he has won two U.S. Amateur titles (1959, 1961). That's why he has won six Masters championships (1963, 1965, 1966, 1972, 1975, 1986), four U.S. Open championships (1962, 1967, 1972, 1980), five U.S. PGA championships (1963, 1971, 1973, 1975, 1980) and three British Open championships (1966, 1970, 1978). That's why he has a total of 70 PGA Tour victories—and many more tournaments in countries from Australia to New Zealand. That's why he's still winning championships on the Senior PGA Tour since joining it in 1990.

Jack's Preparation Process

Jack Nicklaus recognized the critical importance of doing detailed preparatory work prior to an event, prior to a round, prior to every shot he hit from the time he turned professional. He carried a notebook and pencil during a practice round, drawing diagrams of holes, with yardages to various pin placements. Before a round, he'd start hitting balls with a sand wedge, finish his sessions with a driver and hit the same number of balls with the same clubs every time. He would also stick to an exacting pre-swing routine. His near-neurotic, thorough preparation gave him such an advantage over his fellow professionals that he was two to three shots up on the field before tee-off time. In fact, each week, his fellow pros, the press and the gallery would wonder who was going to finish second to Jack.

Even today, Nicklaus usually arrives at the course venue of a major championship a week early to begin his busy work. During practice rounds, he walks the course, mapping out each hole: circled areas designate the best areas to land a tee shot, darkened areas designate the dangerous hazards that lurk off the fairway and off the greens, tiny X's mark the treacherous slopes in a green. By the time Nicklaus completes his prep work, he knows the exact yardage width of every fairway; the size of every green and precisely how many feet in from the front of the putting surface is a particular pin placement; where every safe spot is and where every hazard is—literally every nook and cranny of the course. When his day of mapping out the course is complete, he plays a round in his head at night, seeing himself play every single shot to perfection in his mind's eye.

On the morning of each day's play of the championship, he'll rehearse further on the practice tee. During his regular pre-game routine of going through his bag of clubs, he'll imagine he's playing a shot that he knows he'll have to play during the tournament proper.

When he arrives on the first tee, following a short warm-up session of hitting sand shots and putts, he's totally ready. From the moment he steps up to hit his first drive of the day, he adheres faithfully to another kind of preparation, an orderly pre-shot routine. He checks that his interlocking grip pressure is light enough to keep his forearms relaxed. He makes sure that his arms hang freely from his shoulder sockets, as this encourages a freer swing. He makes sure that his knees are flexed sufficiently enough to feel a springy sensation in them. He makes sure, when driving, that the ball is positioned about an inch behind the left heel—where the club will reach its low point. He also checks that his stance is slightly open, since this allows him to clear his hips more easily on the downswing, opening a clear passageway for the arms to swing the club into the back of the ball.

No one sheds more light on the preciseness of this routine than Seve Ballesteros, the golf superstar who has played often with Nicklaus over the years. This is what he has to say about the master preparer.

For an example of absolute, unvarying meticulousness in setting up to each shot he plays, there is no better model than Jack Nicklaus. The Bear is living proof that a systematic setup enables you to swing and score better. Jack's ability to stick to a disciplined routine through thick and thin, in his driving range work and casual rounds, as well as in the heat of battle, is a major reason why he has so many major championships to his credit. No golfer could ever compile such an awesome record and remain such a factor in his fifties, without absolute self-discipline and systemization in his preparation for every stroke.

There's Jack now, standing directly behind the ball, staring with intense and unshakable concentration down the fairway.

First, he picks the target, the ball's landing area, very specifically; then he selects a mark on the ground a few feet ahead of him directly on that line as his close-up aiming point. Now he programs himself to make the correct swing by running a mental movie of the ball flying on the line and at the trajectory he has so carefully chosen. Next, he carefully steps into the 'golfer's box,' always with the right foot easing into place first, and sets the clubhead behind the ball with its face aligned precisely for the type and

As Seve Ballesteros says, "For an example of absolute, unvarying meticulousness in setting up to each shot he plays, there is no better model than Jack Nicklaus."

degree of sidespin he intends to give the shot. Then, carefully looking back and forth from the ball to his interim target, he eases the club and his body into their final positions. Next, he hovers the clubhead slightly above the ground, waggles it a time or two, then sets it lightly on the ground, with its sweet spot dead square to the ball and target.

Nicklaus is a wonder to watch. The way he works his body into the setup and builds a balanced foundation from the feet upward is really a beautiful sight to any avid golfer. His entire pre-swing process flows as smoothly and cohesively as a piece by Mozart. If you need a model for your own address procedure, you'd have to look long and hard to find a better one.

As good as Nicklaus is today, he's the first to admit how easily a tiny fault can sneak into the pre-swing process and totally foul up his entire game. That's why he used to seek out Grout at every opportunity—and why they always began their lesson by working on posture and the other features of a sound setup. The late Grout believed that the setup accounts for 80 percent of all good ball striking. Nicklaus demonstrated how much respect he has for the setup when he wrote in his magnum opus, *Golf My Way:*

> There are good reasons for my being so methodical about my setup. I think it is the single most important maneuver in golf. It is the only aspect of the swing over which you have 100 percent conscious control. If you set up correctly, there's a good chance you'll hit a reasonable shot, even if you make a mediocre swing. If you set up incorrectly, you'll hit a lousy shot even if you make the greatest swing in the world.

An example of how Nicklaus' preparation paid off took place during the final round of the 1986 Masters, at Augusta National's 16th hole. He was 46 years old at the time, and many had written him off. But when he stood on tee 16, on that final day, he was tied for the lead.

Nicklaus chose a five iron. He stood behind the hole, staring at his target with club in hand. Next, he settled into his shot, looking at the flagstick, then lining up to an interim target. He was ready.

Suddenly, he felt uncomfortable. In this situation, many players would have simply taken a deep breath and swung. Not Nicklaus. He's meticulous and too careful to make such a silly error. He re-teed the ball and began his detailed pre-shot routine all over again in order to give himself the best possible chance of hitting a good shot. He hit a great shot! The ball finished two feet from the hole. He made the putt for birdie. Two holes later he was the champion.

You might not make golf history by generally preparing yourself as meticulously as Jack Nicklaus, but if you copy his setup, you'll give yourself the best chance of cloning his vital swing positions.

The Nicklaus setup: face-on view.

SuperGolf

Nicklaus, in the takeaway, during his early days on the PGA Tour.

Nicklaus at the halfway point in the swing.

Nicklaus at the top of the swing.

Nicklaus in the through-impact position.

Future Famer: Greg Norman

When you watch Greg Norman playing golf today, either on television or at a tournament, it's hard to believe he took up the game late, compared to most of his contemporaries.

As a youngster in Queensland, Australia, Greg loved sports, playing everything from rugby to cricket. But it wasn't until 1970, when he was fifteen, that he borrowed his Mom's clubs and played the Virginia Golf Club course near his home. Norman admits he hit many more bad shots than good ones that day and doesn't remember his score. He does, however, remember that a few solid drives hooked him on the game. After the round he immediately picked up a copy of Jack Nicklaus' *Golf My Way* and began to learn more about the game's technical side.

Three years later, with his handicap down to scratch, he won his first tournament, the Queensland Junior Championship. Three years after that, at age 21, he won his first Australian pro event—the 1976 West Lakes Classic. In 1977, he had one main mission in mind: to prove himself on the European and Asian tours. That year he won the Martini International and finished 20th on the European PGA Tour's Order of Merit. In 1978, Norman won the Fiji Open. He also won the New South Wales Open in Australia, topping that country's money list. The highlights of 1979 were a win in the French Open and the World Matchplay Championship. In winning the Matchplay, he beat Nick Faldo and also Sandy Lyle, who topped that year's Order of Merit. More wins followed.

In 1983, Norman decided to join the United States PGA Tour and test himself against the very toughest golfers in the world. During the period of 1983 to 1990, he won nine titles on the PGA Tour. He also captured the 1986 British Open, and that year Norman lead all four major championships—the Masters, U.S.

Norman's switch to a wide stance (above)
has helped him hit the ball more power-
fully (right).

Open, PGA and British Open—going into the last round. In 1990, he won both the Doral Open and The Memorial and received the Arnold Palmer Award for being the Tour's leading money winner. Not surprisingly, Norman felt on top of the world, and in command of his game.

A year later, his game hit rock bottom. He finished 53rd on the money list. More importantly, he had fallen way down in some key statistical categories, notably driving accuracy and greens in regulation. When Norman looked back at that year, it didn't take him long to realize he needed help. For twenty years he had been relying on good genes, Jack Nicklaus' book and some tips from Australian teacher, Charlie Epp, who in the early years had smoothed out some of the rough edges in Norman's game. It was time for Norman to move forward and build a swing less dependent on perfect timing and rigorous practice, and more likely to stand up to pressure. He needed a new teacher, someone he could trust. After a long search, he chose Claude "Butch" Harmon.

Harmon was honest with Norman. According to Norman, Harmon watched him hit a bag of balls at the TPC at Woodlands in Houston, Texas, and said: "Greg, your stance is too narrow; your footwork is poor; the swing is too long and too steep; and your hips sway on the backswing then slide on the downswing."

At that moment, Norman knew what Nick Faldo and Nick Price must have felt years earlier when they made the commitment to revamp their swings. He knew that if he wanted to play world-class golf, not only would he have to sacrifice some playing time for practice time, but in many ways he would have to start from scratch.

Norman practiced diligently in 1992, and it showed. He climbed to 18th position on the money list, and his overall stats improved. In 1993, Norman finished third on the money list and won the British Open at Royal St. George's. In 1994, he finished second on the money list and proved a lot to the golf world, and himself, by winning The Players Championship with a 24-under-par 264. That was quite a feat, since the venue was the demanding Tournament Players' Championship course at Sawgrass, and because he and his fellow professionals consider this the "fifth major." In 1995, Norman did better yet. He won the Memorial Tournament, the Canon Greater Hartford Open and NEC World Series of Golf to top the money list with $1,654,969. He also won the Vardon Trophy for low-scoring average (69.06) and was voted Player of the Year. In 1996, Norman finished second in the Masters—after leading by six shots going into the final round. However, he learned a lot from the loss.

The key reason for Norman's improved golf is an improved setup position taught to him by Harmon. In fact, Norman is Nicklaus-like in his pre-swing preparation, going through a checklist, making sure that his arms and hands are positioned correctly and that his weight distribution and the width of his stance are also right for him. Norman's right arm is not as extended and tense as it once was, thereby allowing him to make a freer swing and generate more clubhead speed. You need to generate relatively high clubhead speed to produce powerful shots. When gripping, Norman now turns his hands a little more to the right. That's because Harmon showed him how a semi-strong left hand sets the forearm slightly to the right at address, encouraging it to rotate on the backswing and place the club on the proper inside path. Coming down, the stronger grip enhances the releasing action of the arms, hands and club, closing the clubface through impact and promoting a draw.

Norman now positions his hands closer to the target. That's why he now swings the club rhythmically on a more shallow inside path. Formerly, Norman's hands tended to drift behind the ball, thereby causing him to swing from out to in and cut across the ball. The result: that dreaded block shot that Norman hit under pressure.

Just as your hands are the only link to the club, your feet are the only connection to the ground. Therefore, you must start from a solid foundation. On the tee this means setting up with your feet shoulder-width apart, measuring—and this is important—at the inside of the heels. According to Norman, he knew that Ben Hogan played from an extra-wide stance, but he was always thinking so much about positions and swing angles that he never thought to look down at his feet. Harmon educated him on the value of a wide stance, which leads to several improvements: namely, a wider takeaway and swing arc; a shorter, more compact swing; and a turn, rather than slide, of your hips.

At 6'1", it felt natural for Norman to take a narrow stance. And he played pretty well that way. What he didn't know was that compensatory moves and brute strength were allowing him to get away with it—but not all the time. Every now and again, often when it counted most, the narrow stance would fail Norman. He'd swing on such an exaggerated narrow arc that his right wrist would hinge too much at the top, causing the club to drop well below parallel. He'd be in what Harmon calls "the point of no return," unable to bail out and save the swing. So he'd cast the club, slide into impact with his hips too high, reach impact with the clubface open and block the shot to the right of target.

No more. On every swing, he checks his stance. You too can improve by setting your feet farther apart. You will also improve your driving distance and accuracy by taking another page out of Norman's lesson book: Balance your weight evenly on the balls of both feet. In the past, Norman sometimes tended to place 60 percent of his weight on his right foot. This promoted a leg slide rather than a turn.

I think you can see how important the setup position is. Frankly, it predetermines the type of swing you will put on the ball. For that reason, you should take the time to prepare as carefully as Greg Norman does, before you take the club away. Knowing that your address position is technically sound will give you the confidence you need to make an uninhibited, balanced tension-free swing—like Norman's.

2

SWING ALONG WITH SAM

Sam Snead's syrupy tempo, timing and rhythm make him the game's all-time masterful swinger.

"Slammin' Sam" with his trademark palmetto straw hat.

Samuel Jackson Snead was the youngest of six brothers and sisters born to Harry and Laura Snead in the foothills of the Appalachians near Hot Springs, Virginia. The year was 1912. This would prove to be a monumental time in the history of golf, since Byron Nelson and Ben Hogan, two other famous professionals, were born that same year. Together, this trio of Hall of Fame members would win over 175 PGA tournaments, including 20 major championships. Nelson was best known for his superb long-iron play. Hogan's forte was solid ball striking. Snead simply had the smoothest swing in the game.

Sam started his golfing career at age ten, caddying at the Homestead Hotel course, one of his home state's most renowned layouts. The Sneads, like most people from that rural area, didn't have any spare money to spend on golf clubs. In fact, things were so rough that Sam had to be happy with a homemade golf club, made from an old wooden clubhead his brother Homer had discarded, with a buggy whip for a shaft.

Through trial and error, Snead figured out that with this whippy shaft he couldn't swing fast and gain good distance. The slower he swung and the more crack he could generate at the bottom of the swing, the farther the ball would fly. This early club helped Snead develop a smooth, almost lazy-looking swing that, surprisingly, was very powerful indeed.

Snead played golf frequently during his high school days and won several long drive championships. However, his shotmaking prowess never improved all that much until several years later when he took a teaching pro job at the Cascades, a nearby golf resort. This arrangement worked out well for Snead. Between lessons he got to play on the challenging eighteen-hole course and hone his total shotmaking game.

Steady play taught Snead the art of scoring, so much so that, in 1936, he finished third in the Cascades Open, winning

$358.66. Snead felt so good with money in his pocket that he decided to take a train to Pennsylvania. There, he would compete against the likes of Nelson, Hogan, Craig Wood, Paul Runyan, George Fazio and Henry Picard in the Hershey Open for a combined purse of $5,000. Snead shot 67 in the first round. Immediately the whole field, and the golf press corps, began talking excitedly about this country bumpkin with a syrupy swing who had come to town with hay still in his hair. Snead didn't win the tourney. He finished fifth and won $500, plus he earned an endorsement from Dunlop to play their clubs. Brimming with confidence, the young Virginian was ready to try the tour full time.

Snead's first tour victory was the 1937 Oakland Open, which earned him $1,200. Later that year he won the Bing Crosby, St. Paul, Nassau and Miami opens. Snead was launching a career that would see him become the all-time tournament winner, with 81 total PGA victories.

Snead was as much a character as he was a great golfer. One year, early in his career, Snead made the remark that he could beat half the field without his shoes and socks on. So one of the Associated Press writers tried to talk him into playing a round, barefoot, at the Masters. This was an unexpected challenge, since this highly prestigious annual event is played at Georgia's Augusta National—a highly wealthy, very private club with strict rules. It was time to put up or shut up for Snead. Since he was cocky—and a man of his word—he went to the first tee and pulled off his shoes and socks. He then belted a drive 280 yards down the center of the fairway. With only 120 yards to the green, Snead hit his second shot three feet from the pin, then calmly made the putt for a birdie three. The grass under Snead's feet reminded him of his childhood days, when he chased rabbits, hunted squirrels and climbed trees with bare feet. Snead shot 68, while most of the field were shooting in the low 70s. He was unaware, however, that he was getting into trouble.

Gene Sarazen, whom Snead idolized, came running out of the clubhouse and told him that he had set golf back ten years. After all, the pros were trying to get away from the image of hillbillies and gamblers. By playing barefoot in the Masters, Snead certainly hurt their image. Sarazen's comment had such an effect on Snead that from then on he always conducted himself as a perfect gentleman on the course.

When you look at Snead's career, a lot of thoughts come to mind: smooth swing, the palmetto straw hat that was Snead's trademark for over 60 years, the sidesaddle putting stroke that he employed until it was banned, 81 career wins, the U.S. Open that Snead never won. It wasn't as though he didn't have a chance to win the Open. You don't play for four decades like Sam Snead did and not have a few chances to win the Open. The way Snead lost a couple of Opens is what most golfers remember.

In the summer of 1939, the U.S. Open was played at Spring Mill (Philadelphia Country Club) in Pennsylvania. Snead had posted two really good rounds, shooting 68 the first day, 71 the second. In the third round his putter turned sour, and he shot 73. All the same, Snead was still in good position to make his move on the leader and win the coveted title.

Snead played well on the fourth and final day. His drives were long and straight, his irons fell close to the pin, and his putting was much better than the day before. After 16 holes Snead figured that if he scored pars on numbers 17 and 18, he would win the Open and tie Ralph Guldahl's 1937 low scoring record of 281. Snead wanted the record as well as the trophy, so he took out his driver on the 17th hole and blasted away. Snead hit the perfect shot, leaving himself with only a short iron to the green.

However, his approach shot flew off line before bounding into the heavy rough near the edge of the green.

That is where Snead's troubles started. His chip shot barely got onto the green, so he had to settle for two putts and a bogie score. What happened next Snead has replayed in his mind a million times. The 18th hole at Spring Mill is a long par five with trees and deep rough lining both sides of the fairway. Snead hooked his drive into the rough guarding the left side of the fairway, leaving himself an extremely difficult second shot. The ball was almost totally covered in grass. But Snead, thinking he needed birdie to win, gambled by trying to smash a two-wood shot far down the fairway— or onto the green. That wasn't to be. He failed to make solid contact with the ball and hit it into a fairway bunker. Worse yet, the ball now lay between two layers of sod. Snead needed a miracle. That wasn't to be either. His eight-iron shot got the ball out of the trap, but only just barely. All he could do was swing as hard as he could and hope that he could hit the ball solidly. Again he hit a bad recovery shot; the ball found its way into a greenside bunker. Snead got the ball safely out but left himself a 20-foot putt for six. After studying the putt from all angles, he hit the ball three feet past the hole. Shaken, he lost his train of thought and missed the next putt. Snead had scored a triple bogey eight on the final hole of the Open. Make no mistake, an overconfident Snead had choked. Snead knew it, and never forgot it. Even now, he'll tell you, a day doesn't go by that he doesn't replay the last hole at Spring Mill.

In 1947, at the St. Louis Country Club, another nightmare occurred for Snead in the U.S. Open Championship. Snead lost an 18-hole playoff to Lou Worsham after bogeying the last two holes. Believe it or not, that disaster was highlighted by missing a thirty-inch putt on the final green to tie Worsham's score of 69. Snead was just about to putt when Worsham asked the referee to measure which ball was farther from the cup. After much delay, the referee decided that Snead's ball was half an inch outside

Worsham's ball. Snead, therefore, had to putt first. He became so upset by this apparent display of gamesmanship he missed the putt. Worsham made his, so poor Snead lost another heartbreaking U.S. Open.

It's important to note that if Snead had shot 69 in the last round of every U.S. Open he played in (which he was very capable of doing), he would have won the Open nine times. It's important to note, too, that although this one major championship eluded him, he won three Masters titles, a British Open and three PGA championships. Sam Snead has also been on winning World Cup and Ryder Cup teams. He has been the Tour's leading money winner and leading scorer, and he's still in the record books as the oldest individual winner. At the age of 52 years, ten months and eight days, he won the 1965 Greater Greensboro Open. He has even shot 59.

Snead was still winning tournaments in the 1980s, when he and Gardner Dickinson won the Legends of Golf, which evolved into the Senior PGA Tour. If there had been a Senior Tour when Snead turned 50, the number of victories he would have won would have been mind-boggling.

So Sam Snead never captured the U.S. Open. His other great golf feats and gorgeous swing captured the hearts of millions of golfers around the world. His rhythmic swing has stood the test of time, proving that his fundamentals were sound. There are, however, many other elements of his address, backswing and downswing to study and learn from. So let's examine those vital cornerstones that the "Slammin' Sam" swing was built upon.

Snead's Smooth Swing Method

When Sam Snead set up to the ball, the beautiful balance and grace he possessed became immediately apparent. Snead gave the impression that there was never any tension in his body, that his body was oiled, loose as a goose, ready to spring into action and deliver another long drive straight down the middle of the fairway. He made it look easy because he always put his body in a balanced position before he made that gorgeous long swing of his.

For Snead, this adherence to balance started in the grip. He thought that, because the hands controlled the clubface, you must have them perfectly balanced on the club's handle before starting the swing. This wasn't always the case. Early on, Snead fought a terrible hook shot that flew low off the clubface, then darted dead left. Snead tried all sorts of remedies for this shot-making problem, such as opening his alignment and moving the ball back in his stance. One day Snead noticed that when he moved his right hand more on top of the club (so that the "V" formed by his thumb and forefinger pointed at his right shoulder, rather than outside it), the ball flew straight. Still, Snead complained that the new grip felt downright strange and uncomfortable. He even worried about going back to the old comfortable grip when the pressure was on during a tournament. But he stuck with the new grip, and after a few weeks it felt okay.

To assume a grip like Snead's, let the club's handle run diagonally across your left hand from the base of the forefinger to a point just below the pad of the palm. Rest the thumb of the left hand down the right center of the handle. Let the handle rest along the base of the fingers of the right hand. Snead discovered that gripping the club with more of a finger hold than a palm hold allowed him to release the club more powerfully through the impact zone. To enhance control, Snead had the little finger of his right hand rest between the first and second fingers of his left hand. He also held the club with a light pressure as though he were holding a bird—not too light, not too firm. On a scale of 1 to 10, about 6. Good advice.

In the setup position, Snead always wanted his shoulders to match his feet, because this puts the body in the ultimate position to strike the ball solidly. If he was playing his normal gentle draw, his feet and shoulders would be aimed to the right of target, just slightly. If, however, the shot called for a slight fade, Snead would aim his shoulders a bit left of target, then align his feet parallel to the shoulder line. This address promotes an outside-to-inside swing path that, in turn, produces a shot that starts its flight down the left side of the fairway, then fades back to the center of the fairway. For your purposes, if you're not playing some sort of specialty shot, set your feet and shoulders parallel to an imaginary line running from the ball to the target. The width of your stance should be slightly wider than your shoulders, like Snead's was when playing the driver.

The knees should be bent slightly so that the "caps" cover the knots of your shoelaces. When you flex the knees too much, weight falls on the heels, making it difficult for the body to coil and uncoil. Snead believed that his body moved more freely when his weight was on the balls of his feet. More good advice. The upper body should be tilted forward from the hips, with your back pockets sticking out, not down. Most golfers bend more from the waist than from the hips, causing the spine to be hunched over and out of position. Snead's arms were extended but not stiff. This tension-free arms position will allow you to generate faster clubhead speed. Don't look at the ball with both eyes. If like Snead, your left eye is dominant, turn your head to the right before swinging to get a better look at the ball.

On the backswing Snead employed a one-piece takeaway, meaning that the shoulders, arms, hands and wrists work as a team to take the club away smoothly. Think of the words *low* and

SuperGolf

Snead swings the club back on an inside path.

Notice how Snead starts the club back low to the ground.

Snead keeps the club virtually parallel to the ground at the halfway point in the swing.

Snead's head stays rock steady as he swings the club up.

SuperGolf

At this point in the swing, Snead's left arm is perfectly straight—one reason why he guided the club back on precisely the same path, time after time.

Snead next concentrates on rotating his left shoulder under his chin.

Here, the majority of Snead's weight is on his right instep and heel.

When Snead reaches the top, the clubshaft parallels the imaginary ball-target line. Snead has always believed that setting the club in this position gives you the best chance of hitting a powerfully accurate shot.

SuperGolf

Snead's buckling knees set him in position to employ a "late hit."

Now weight starts shifting to Snead's left foot.

Snead's right wrist is still cocked, meaning he's waiting until the last split second of the swing to unleash his power.

Snead keeps his head behind the ball to promote a powerful upswing hit.

SuperGolf

Snead in his classic follow-through position.

Snead: hitting against a firm left side, and applying the sweet spot of the clubface to the back center portion of the ball.

Snead turning through the ball.

Snead's classic on-balance finish position.

slow when starting the swing to help you make a smooth, streamlined takeaway action. When driving, the clubhead should stay low to the ground for the first 12 to 18 inches of the swing. This move promotes a wide arc and even tempo. If you jerk the club away, the swing's arc will become overly narrow and the speed of your tempo will quicken. These faults will usually result in a weak slice shot.

Snead was extremely flexible, so he had a tremendous body coil that enabled him to set the club in the classic parallel position at the top of his swing. Make sure that the club goes as far back as you can coil, using your upper body, not your arms and hands, to control the motion. If you take the club back using exaggerated arms-hands action, it will swing past the parallel position and cost you power. Power is produced by coiling the body. As Snead swung the club to the top, his weight shifted to the heel of his right foot. If you're fully coiled, you'll feel extra weight on the inside portion of your right heel. If weight shifts to the outside of your right foot, your body isn't balanced. It also proves that you swayed instead of turned. This fault leads to mishits of one kind or another.

All smooth swingers—not just Snead—look like they have a slight pause at the top of the backswing. In actuality, the golfer isn't pausing. He is allowing the club to change directions and is now ready to start down. Snead's downswing was so beautiful and smooth it appeared that he was hardly swinging. The truth is, Snead developed a tremendous amount of clubhead speed at the bottom of the arc. How? The secret of Snead's power was that he didn't uncock his wrists until after the wrists passed his right pocket. This allowed him to wait until the last vital split second of the downswing to whip the club into the ball. Most golfers make the mistake of uncocking the wrists early in the downswing. Frankly, this is why they never attain the powerful "late hit." In

Snead's swing, the sharp angle formed by his left arm and shaft was maintained until almost impact—stored energy waiting to explode.

When Snead was playing winning golf, he started the downswing by shifting his weight to his left side. Next, the hips rotated in a counterclockwise direction, causing the club to drop down into the hitting slot automatically. Again, there was no conscious manipulation of the club with the hands. Once the club dropped down, all Snead did was keep shifting and rotating his lower body. He only had to keep his head down and wait for his wrists to uncock. At that point—impact—the sweet spot of the clubface would be driven into the center back portion of the ball.

Snead had one of the most relaxed finish positions of all time, owing to his tension-free balanced swing. He never forced the swing; he simply swung the force—with powerful grace. A practice drill that Snead used to find the ultimate balance point and tempo in his swing is one that you should try: Swing as hard as you can (without a ball) and try to stay balanced. If you lose your balance, gear back a notch each time you swing until you discover your most controlled swing tempo.

FUTURE FAMER: PAYNE STEWART

Payne Stewart is the nineties version of Sam Snead. Granted, Stewart hasn't won nearly as many tournaments as Snead. Nevertheless, his technically sound, pretty swing has earned him over 7 million dollars in prize money and nine tour titles (including two major championships). Stewart ranks in the top ten on the PGA Tour's all-time money list. And it's a sure bet that he's not through winning yet. So he's well on his way to becoming a Hall of Famer.

Stewart grew up in Springfield, Missouri, a town that has had two Masters champions, Horton Smith and Herman Kaiser. Springfield is so golf crazy that two of its city courses are named

Payne Stewart: the PGA Tour's smoothest swinger.

after its favorite golfing sons, Horton Smith and Payne Stewart. Hickory Hills Country Club, a beautiful and challenging course, is where Stewart cut his golfing teeth. His father, Bill, won the club championship many times and later went on to win the Missouri State Amateur. Bill Stewart was not only known for his great golfing abilities; he was also a flashy dresser. Payne, who dresses in knickers, must have taken a page out of his father's book on fashion.

Stewart had excelled at SMU in Dallas, where he became a second-team All American during his senior year. However, it took Stewart four tries before he finally got his PGA Tour card and another three years before he won his first event, the 1982 Quad Cities Open.

During most of the 1980s, Stewart's fellow professionals called him "Avis" because he had so many seconds. All this teasing was put to rest in 1989 when Stewart shot a final round score of 67 at Kemper Lakes in Illinois to win the PGA Championship over Mike Reid. Two years later, Stewart won the U.S. Open Championship, beating Scott Simpson in an 18-hole playoff.

Payne Stewart doesn't just have a Hall of Fame swing. He has a Hall of Fame heart as well. After winning the 1987 Bay Hill Classic, Stewart donated the first place check to Florida's Arnold Palmer Hospital, in memory of his dad who had just lost his battle with cancer.

Stewart also has the determination and competitive spirit of a Hall of Famer. In the 1991 Ryder Cup matches, played at South Carolina's Kiawah Island Ocean course, Stewart won two out of three matches in the best ball competition, pairing up with Mark Calcavecchia. Stewart is the perfect team player, always rooting his teammates on to victory. In the 1993 Ryder Cup, played at The Belfry in England, Stewart and Ray Floyd fought hard to win two team matches. Plus, Stewart beat Mark James in a critical singles match. Stewart's play inspired the rest of the team to buckle down and take home the coveted Cup.

Along with Stewart's will to win, it's his super swing that earns him victories around the world. His swing is so smooth (poetry in motion!) that, by looking at his body, you can't tell if he's swinging a driver or a wedge. Stewart's extension action on the backswing is exceptional. His right arm stays perfectly straight as the club goes back, creating a big arc. At the top, his body is coiled to the maximum, all set to unleash the club solidly into the ball. At the start of the downswing, the right elbow drops down close to the body, while the club falls into the perfect hitting position.

Through impact, Stewart stays behind the ball and hits against a firm left side. To help establish good balance and a smooth tempo, Stewart hits a lot of balls with his feet together. If you can hit solid shots with your feet together, you are swinging at the right speed. If, however, you try to hit the ball too hard, you'll feel yourself lose your balance.

It is fun to watch Stewart, whether it's on television coming down the stretch in a PGA tournament or on the range hitting balls. The next time you see Stewart play, just watch his body during the swing. Forget what the club is doing. Don't watch the ball's flight either. After just a few minutes, you'll pick up some vital pointers on "swinging within yourself" that will hopefully stay with you for a long time to come.

3

SOLID IMPACT

Ben Hogan's on-plane swing has always been the secret to his powerful ball striking.

Ben Hogan in his traditional white linen cap, staring intently at the target.

"Bantam Ben" was Ben Hogan's nickname, but he was a giant among golf's greats. He studied the shot at hand as intently as a chess champion studies the board before his next move. Under the white linen cap he traditionally wore, the wheels of his wise golfing brain were always turning. Hogan's stare said that. Hogan was blessed with a rare golfing mind. As for his swing, that has been called the most perfect of all time. Hogan developed it by hitting practice balls until his hands bled. Hogan was the first touring professional to practice after the round. No matter how well he played, he'd show up to hit balls. No one got more satisfaction out of hitting solid golf shots than Ben Hogan. No one got more pleasure out of seeking technical perfection. Hogan's game was a model of consistency, and he never finished out of the top ten in U.S. Open play between 1940 and 1950. In Ryder Cup competition he was undefeated.

Benjamin William Hogan was born in Dublin, Texas, on August 13, 1912, the second son, and the third child, of Chester and Clara Hogan. His father committed suicide when he was nine years old. This event forced Hogan to grow up in a hurry and help the family. Finding he could make more money caddying than selling newspapers, Hogan found employment at Glen Garden Golf Course. A young boy named Byron Nelson was already caddying at "The Garden" when Hogan showed up looking for work. These two hungry youngsters would turn out to be golfing heroes.

Hogan was a natural lefty. But since there weren't many left-handed golfers around to give him their used clubs, he learned to play right-handed. When Hogan wasn't caddying, he was on the practice range. Because he didn't have any formal training on how to swing the club, Hogan tried to copy some of the better players' swings. However, he soon realized that if he was ever going to make it as a golfer, he needed to develop his own style.

Turning pro at nineteen, with $100 in his hip pocket and a duck hook in his bag, Hogan set out for the Winter Tour of 1933. It didn't take long for him to realize that his game was out of control. He couldn't find the fairway. After a month, Hogan was broke and headed home to Texas. He practiced for months, trying to find the answer to his swing problems. He was able to save enough money to rejoin the Tour, but again things didn't go his way. Determined, not discouraged, Hogan returned to Texas and again became a slave to the practice range. He practiced from sunup to sundown, hoping to stumble on a foolproof swing secret. Hogan always thought the answer to his problem was "in the dirt." That means if you keep hitting balls, by the hour, day, month and year, you will eventually dig the answer out of the dirt. He knew that if he practiced more than anyone else, he would eventually make it. Learning this way is a slow and tedious process. After three years of intense practice, his game started to show improvement.

In 1936, Hogan qualified for the U.S. Open but missed the 36 hole cut. Hogan knew he had to learn how to take his game from the practice tee to the course and have his swing hold up under pressure. Hoping the third time would be the charm, he rejoined the Tour in 1937. Finishing third in Lake Placid and tenth in the Canadian Open boosted Hogan's confidence.

With his wife Valerie at his side, and a little over $1,000, Hogan set his sights on the Winter Tour of 1938. Inconsistency plagued him throughout the Southern California tournaments. By the time the Hogans reached Oakland they had only $85 to their names, and Hogan was at the crossroads of his career. At this point he must have thought: "Play well and you can stay out on Tour; play poorly and you're back to Texas looking for a new profession." Hogan was nervous before he teed off, but he was determined to play well. Playing every shot with deliberation and purpose, Hogan shot a 66 and was the first round leader. Steady play earned Hogan a third place finish and a check for $385. He had proven to himself that he had the game to play on the Tour.

In the spring of 1940, he won his first tournament, the North and South Open. Hogan was the talk of the Tour that year. He won three more times. He was the Tour's leading money winner and had the lowest scoring average. In 1941, Hogan won five times and finished second eleven times. He again was the Tour's leading money winner and captured the Vardon Trophy for the second straight season. The 1942 Tour season held great promise for Hogan, but halfway through the year the war called, and Hogan entered the Army Air Corps.

Sam Snead and Byron Nelson were dominating the Tour when Hogan rejoined in 1945. Everyone was curious to see whether Hogan could recapture the number one spot. It didn't take Hogan long to silence his critics. He picked up where he left off. Over the next four and a half years, he won 35 tournaments, including the PGA Championship in 1946 and 1948. The 1948 U.S. Open was held on one of Hogan's favorite courses, the Riviera Country Club. Hogan played Riviera so well that the press nicknamed the course "Hogan's Alley." Shooting a 276, Hogan broke the U.S. Open record.

In 1949, Ben and Valerie were traveling back to Texas after a tournament when a bus struck their car head on. He probably saved his wife's life by throwing himself over her body right before impact. He suffered a double fracture of the pelvis, a broken left ankle and a broken collarbone and nearly died from the blood clots that formed during surgery. It appeared his golfing days were over. The doctors said he would be fortunate if he could ever walk again, much less play golf. Obviously, the doctors didn't know the fire of will that burned in Ben Hogan's heart. After three months, he was able to go outside. Later that summer, with legs covered in bandages from thigh to ankle, he started practicing. Everyone doubted he could come back. Everyone, that is, except Hogan.

Just 11 months after the accident, Hogan electrified the sporting world. After four rounds, he was tied with Sam Snead for first place in the Los Angeles Open. On weak and battered legs, Hogan lost in a playoff, but he won the hearts of golfers all around the country for his courage and intestinal fortitude. He had proven his point—Ben was back. After the accident his desire to win was even greater. It was as if an even stronger competitive fire had been sewn into his body along with the stitches that healed his broken legs. He won the 1950 U.S. Open and the 1951 Masters and, two months later, captured his third U.S. Open title.

The 1953 season was Ben Hogan's greatest year; he won the Masters, the U.S. Open and the British Open—an unmatched feat that many consider more difficult than Bobby Jones winning the Grand Slam. Hogan's triple sweep was done in an era of many great players, and it earned him a ticker tape parade down Broadway in New York City.

The highlight of 1953 was Hogan's first and only trip to play in the British Open. The site of the championship was Carnoustie, Scotland. The weather made the course play different each day. Hogan's game was up to nature's challenge. Hogan opened with a 73, and a second round 71 found him two strokes behind the leader. The third day Hogan battled the wind and cold to shoot a phenomenal score of 70. The Scotsmen were out in full force to watch the great Hogan on the final day. He didn't let them down. His winning 282 was a remarkable performance. He mastered the Carnoustie links as nobody had ever done before. It was a fitting climax to that wonderful summer of 1953.

Hogan had many good years afterward, but winning the U.S. Open one more time would have made life sweeter. He had already won the U.S. Open four times, and nobody had ever won five. It looked like he was a sure winner in 1955, until an unknown pro from Iowa named Jack Fleck charged late with a run of birdies and forced a playoff. Hogan lost the playoff, shooting a 72 to Fleck's 69—one of the greatest upsets in the history of sports. In 1956, needing two pars on the last two holes to tie

Cary Middlecoff for the U.S. Open, Hogan missed a thirty-inch par putt on the 71st hole and had to settle for second place. The last chance Hogan had of winning his fifth Open Championship was in 1960 at Cherry Hills. Hogan was closing fast on Arnold Palmer, until a gambling shot he hit on the 71st hole found the water. Another chance to win a fifth Open blown.

Nobody hit a golf ball like Ben Hogan. The force that he applied to the ball was different from most players of that era. His shots had a different sound and trajectory, too. But the curve of the ball was the same every time. A soft left-to-right fade was Hogan's bread-and-butter shot. Still today, years after he retired, top teaching professionals use Hogan's swing as a model for golfers to imitate. Let's now find out what is so special about the Hogan technique.

Ben's Powerful Swing Technique

Hogan's masterful power swing started with a unique grip. In assuming his left hand grip, allow the club's handle to rest under the heel pad of the palm and lie directly across the top joint of the forefinger. Next, as Hogan advised, crook the forefinger around the handle and you'll discover that you can maintain a firm grip on it by supporting it with just the muscles of that finger and the muscles of the pad of the palm. Now close the remainder of your left hand around the club. The "V" that is formed by the thumb and the forefinger should be pointing toward your right eye. There is pressure in the last three fingers of the left hand. Hogan felt that the pressure in the last three fingers of the left hand firmed up the left side through the swing, kept the club from slipping and helped maintain a flat left wrist at impact.

The right hand is then placed on the club so that the club is across the top joint of the first four fingers, but below the palm. The middle two fingers of the right hand must control the club.

The "V" that is formed by the first finger and thumb of the right hand points toward your chin. To make sure your hands work as a unit, place the little finger of the right hand between the first finger and middle finger of the left hand. The grip pressure is firm, but not tight.

After Jack Fleck beat Hogan to win the 1955 Open, *Life* magazine paid Hogan $25,000 to tell the world about the *secret* that was responsible for his success. The secret that Hogan had discovered after many hours on the practice range had two key elements: The left hand was turned about an inch to the left of the center of the club. This placed the left thumb on top of the club, instead of on the right side. The second element was in the left wrist. In the early stage of the takeaway, the left wrist was cupped backward and inward, so it would form a slight "V" at the top of the backswing. The clubface was open. Now, with all the force Hogan could muster, he could close the clubface on the downswing and not worry about hooking the ball. This should only be tried by the serious golfer. It is a move that took the great Ben Hogan years to perfect and is not for everyone.

When setting up, Hogan knew that if his arms were close to his body, he would stay connected during the swing. To get the correct feeling of this, Hogan practiced hitting balls with a towel under his arms. When his arms moved away from the body, the towel would fall to the ground. You should try this drill.

At address, Hogan's elbows were pointed inward. The left elbow pointed toward his left hip bone; the right elbow pointed toward his right hip bone. This positioning of elbows to hips linked Hogan's upper and lower body together. With a driver, Hogan's feet were slightly wider than shoulder width. Using this particular width base helps you maintain good balance through the swing and, more importantly, gives you traction. Hogan set his right foot perpendicular to the target line. He angled his left foot out 20 degrees. His right foot position allowed him to make a stronger body coil on the backswing. His left foot position allowed him to clear his hips more freely on the downswing. Hogan favored a forward ball position when driving and played it about an inch inside his left heel to promote a powerful upswing hit.

Hogan was aware that how he set his spine would influence the plane of his swing. If the spine is slightly erect, the shoulders will turn on the correct plane. When the spine is tilted forward, and the shoulders are humped over, the plane is too steep. If the spine is too straight, you haven't bent enough from the hips. When setting up, Hogan's knees were bent slightly. More importantly, one of his secrets to making solid contact at impact was maintaining that flex throughout the swing. In trying to swing on plane, he visualized a sheet of glass resting on his shoulders and tilting downward toward the ball. If his arms lifted up, the imaginary glass would be broken. If the shoulder turn was too flat or rotary, the club would be below the imaginary sheet. Ideally, when the arms approach hip level on the backswing, they should be moving parallel with the plane and should remain parallel with it at the top of the backswing.

When you have a setup like Hogan's and you start back with the hands, arms, shoulders and hips coiling around the spine, the club will be swung on the correct plane. The backswing starts with the hands moving slightly before the arms. Once the hands move so far, the arms then start to swing. The swinging of the arms causes the shoulders to start turning. The action works like a link chain; each link provides strength to the next link. When a link is broken, the chain has lost its strength. Stay linked.

Hogan's shoulders coiled well past the 90 degree mark because he was very flexible in his upper body. On the backswing, try to get your left shoulder to rotate under your chin and your back to the target. Once the shoulders can't turn any more, it is time to stop.

Hogan kept his left arm straight on the backswing for two chief reasons:

1. It served as a brace and allowed him to set the club perfectly on plane at the top.
2. It helped him maintain a wide swing arc—another of his vital power secrets.

Hogan's hip-clearing action, on the downswing, allowed him to generate high clubhead speed and hit the ball powerfully.

Hogan's downswing started by turning his hips to the left, setting off a powerful chain reaction. Once your hips have turned back to the left, your body weight moves from your right foot to your left foot. This shifting action moves the hips out of the way, so the arms can accelerate the club into the ball. According to

Notice how Hogan keeps his left foot on the ground—one of his secrets to good balance.

SuperGolf

Hogan, the faster you clear the hips, the faster your clubhead speed and the farther the ball flies.

Hogan had a picture-perfect finish. In the finish, your body should be balanced with the majority of your weight on the left side. The left foot stays virtually flat on the ground. Only the toe end of your right foot should be touching the ground. Because Hogan used his lower body to lead the downswing, his left foot

Observe Hogan's fluid shoulder and hip actions.

didn't spin out or roll over. Hogan's spine was straight, and his hands were behind his left shoulder—truly a classic finish that comes only to those who swing within themselves.

Try to practice Hogan's picture-perfect setup and swing. And if you have problems, remember: The answer is *in the dirt.*

FUTURE FAMER: JOHN DALY

Every once in a while a player comes along who captures the golfing world's imagination. It happened in 1930 when Bobby Jones won the Grand Slam, in 1945 when Byron Nelson won 18 tournaments and in 1962 when Jack Nicklaus beat Arnold Palmer in the U.S. Open and it is happening again. John Daly is a modern-day folk hero, a real Paul Bunyan in spikes, one of a select few to have won his second major championship before age 30. Just the thought of his name makes any round ball shudder.

Daly started playing golf when he was four years old, with a couple of old Jack Nicklaus clubs his father had cut down to his size. The clubs were heavy, and Daly had to swing over his head for power. This early training probably helped him build the long power swing he employs today.

After beating all the juniors around Fredericksburg, Virginia, Daly turned his attention to the adults. At age thirteen he won the men's spring championship at Lake of the Woods Golf Course. When the adults couldn't beat him on the course, they did the next best thing. They banned him for the next five years from all their men's tournaments. They may have thought this punishment would teach Daly a lesson, but it only enhanced his desire to win. The Dalys moved often when he was in high school, so golf took the place of a faithful friend. He won the Missouri State High School Championship in his junior year and the Arkansas State High School Championship his senior year.

John Daly's exceptionally strong body turn and extra-long backswing allow him to propel the ball powerfully into the air.

After three years at the University of Arkansas, Daly left college to concentrate on his game full time. In 1990, he won on the Hogan Tour and that fall qualified for the PGA Tour. Nothing, however, had prepared Daly for what was in store for him the second week of August 1991.

Being the ninth alternate for the PGA Championship usually means you can look for another place to play that weekend. Fate was on Daly's side, however, because players were dropping out right and left. When Nick Price withdrew at the last second, Daly was in the field of contenders. Perhaps so many players dropped out because they were afraid of the Pete Dye course. Crooked Stick, located in Carmel, Indiana, measures 7,289 yards from the tips—a true monster. The fairways are narrow, and the rough bordering them was purposely allowed to grow high that year. Since Daly got the call that he was in the championship only one day before it began, he didn't have time to play a practice round. Daly didn't know where the trouble was, so he fearlessly hit his driver on the par-four and par-five holes. He focused in on the fairways and greens, not the trouble, and shot a three-under par 69 the first day. Many onlookers and television commentators thought Daly's big drives would cause him problems, but he had his power swing under control. On Friday, the second day of the championship, he shot a solid 67 to take the lead. Daly had everything to win and nothing to lose. He used only one swing thought throughout the tournament: "grip it and rip it." Once in the lead, Daly wasn't about to give it up. He won that 1991 PGA Championship by three strokes over Bruce Lietzke. Daly had gone from a complete unknown to a major star in one week.

In the summer of 1995, John Daly captured his second major championship, the British Open. Since World War II, Johnny Miller, Jack Nicklaus and Tom Watson had been the only golfers to win two major tournaments before the age of thirty. Now

John Daly's name was added to that list. No one knows when golf was first played on St. Andrews. Some believe it was around 1562. But one thing is certain: the Old Course had never seen a golfer like John Daly. His drives were long, so long that he drove six of the par fours. There wasn't a par five that he couldn't reach in two shots. Sometimes he could reach the green with a middle iron. The key to his victory was his ability to hit the fairways. The course has a multitude of deep pot bunkers, so Daly had to hit the tee ball long and straight.

In setting up for the power drive, Daly has a strong grip. There have been many long hitters with a strong grip, most notably Arnold Palmer. To strengthen your grip, turn both hands to the right, so the "V"s formed by your thumbs and forefingers point up at your right shoulder.

Daly's body coil on the backswing is incredibly powerful. Turning his feet out 25 degrees at address is the secret to his big turn. With his hips and shoulders coiling to the max, his upper body is ready to unleash power in the downswing. No one has ever made as big a body turn as John Daly—or swung the club back as far. You might not be able to turn as far back as Daly, but challenge yourself and your body to keep stretching back. The more you turn, the more powerfully you will unwind your body and the farther you will hit the ball.

Here's a drill that will increase your flexibility and enhance your body turn: Take two or three clubs and hold them together. Next, take your setup position. Raise the clubs about twelve inches off the ground. Make a slow backswing. Once you reach the top, pause for three seconds. Swing down. Repeat several times.

The next time you are outside and hear a sound from the sky, look up. It could be John Daly's long ball on its way to the PGA Golf Hall of Fame.

4

STRAIGHT DOWN THE MIDDLE

Arnold Palmer still drives the ball with pinpoint accuracy.

Arnold Palmer: He's still considered Mr. Golf.

Arnold Palmer just may be the most loved man in sports. As Lee Trevino says, "More people watch Arnie load his clubs in his car than watch the leaders at some tournaments." Everybody—from the average Sunday hacker to the seasoned pro to the elderly retired couple in Kansas sitting in front of their television watching golf—adores "Arnie." And they should. He epitomizes the American dream; the young boy who came up the hard way and, against the odds, made it big in the land of opportunity. He is the man who brought the galleries to American courses to see him smash drives straight down the fairway and ram long putts into the hole. His loyalty to the game and his swashbuckling style of play were responsible for revitalizing the British Open in the early 1960s. Palmer has always been a modest champion who was also always gracious in defeat. He has played with presidents and kings, Joe Louis and Jackie Gleason. He is famous enough to have been painted by Norman Rockwell, and rich enough to own his own jet. Yet he never pushes an autograph seeker aside and, furthermore, wouldn't think of charging money for his signature as so many modern-day athletes do. His schedule is full, but he always finds time to visit the sick in hospitals and cheer them up. In fact, he founded the Arnold Palmer Hospital for Children and Women. He's a superb family man. He's a great golfer. God help the golf world the day Arnold Palmer passes on, for there will be left a mighty gap that shall never be filled.

Arnold Daniel Palmer was born September 10, 1929, in Latrobe, Pennsylvania. He lived on the golf course of the Latrobe Country Club, at a time when families with money lived in town, at a time, too, when golf pros were thought of as servants. Palmer's father, Deacon, was the original greenskeeper at the Latrobe Country Club. Then, during the Great Depression, when money was tight for the club, he was asked to take on the job of golf pro as well. Things were so rough at the time that only the kitchen and living room of their home had heat, thanks to a fire-place. Young Arnold, of course, hung tough as he has done through his entire golfing career.

At the age of three, Arnold's father made him a set of clubs. However, the opportunities to improve his game were very lim-ited. He was only allowed to play on the Latrobe course in the early morning before the members arrived or in the evening after they had left. Still, by the age of seven, he broke 100 for 18 holes. Palmer quickly improved and started to shoot lower scores. He twice won the Pennsylvania State High School Championship. His game was good enough to earn him a schol-arship to Wake Forest. Palmer dropped out of college, joined the Coast Guard, returned to college, dropped out of college, became a paint salesman.

The turning point in Palmer's life came in 1954, when he won the United States Amateur championship. This boosted his confi-dence and encouraged him to turn pro. Once Palmer announced his decision, Wilson Sporting Goods agreed to pay him $5,000 per year to endorse their clubs. Late that same year, he married Winifred Walzer, whom he's been married to ever since. In 1955, Palmer shot rounds of 64, 67, 64 and 70 to win his first tourna-ment, the Canadian Open. He finished the year in 22nd place on the money list. In 1956, he won the Panama Open, the Colombia Open, the Insurance City Open and the Eastern Open. In 1957, he won the Houston Open, the Azalea Open, the Rubber City Open and the San Diego Open.

In 1958, Palmer brought his game to a new dimension and entered the world of superstardom. He won his first "major" championship, the Masters Tournament, and ended the year in first place on the money list. He and wife Winnie could finally afford to give up their sleep-in trailer and stay in hotel rooms when on the road. They had enough money to buy a house, too.

Palmer would go on to win six other major professional championships. He won the Masters three more times (1960, 1962 and 1964), the United States Open once (1960) and the British Open twice (1961 and 1962). The only major championship that has eluded Arnold Palmer is the PGA. In total, Palmer has won 61 PGA Tour events.

With the help of Mark McCormack, the CEO of International Management Group, and his own Arnold Palmer Enterprises, Palmer has been able to wheel his victories and personality into lucrative endorsement contracts with such companies as Cadillac, Pennzoil, Textron, PaineWebber, GTE and Rolex. To Palmer, however, it's not about money. He loves golf for golf. That's why he started the Palmer Course Design Company in 1979 and joined the Senior PGA Tour the following year. Since that time, he has created some wonderful courses around the world and, after winning the first senior event he entered, the 1980 PGA Senior Championship, has chalked up 11 more victories.

Although Palmer was a tremendous putter during his winning days on the PGA Tour, his forte has always been driving. For a long time, he has been a powerfully accurate tee-ball hitter. Of course, his reputation for long, straight driving began in 1960, when he teed it up for the final round of the U.S. Open, seven strokes behind the leaders. This is how Palmer described his opening tee shot that sparkling summer day in Denver:

On the fourth round of the 1960 Open, I tried a shot that I'd missed three times in three rounds. I tried it again not because I'd failed—or because I like failure—but because I was convinced that it was necessary to win the tournament.

A bold shot?

Yes.

But you must play boldly to win.

A reckless shot?

No.

In eighteen years of tournament golf I feel that I've never tried a shot that I couldn't make.

My own needs were deeply driven ones: I could not retreat from a challenge. If the chance was there and if—no matter how difficult it appeared—it meant winning, I was going to take it. It was the sweetness of risk that I remembered, and not its dangers.

But perhaps it was not until the U.S. Open at Cherry Hills that I put it all together, philosophically as well as physically. For not until that summer day in 1960 did it become apparent to me how boldness might influence not just a hole, but an entire round, an entire tournament and even an entire golfing career.

It began, really, on the first tee of the last round at Cherry Hills. The hole was 346 yards long, guarded on the left by an irregular line of poplars and pines and on the right by a ditch that the membership had practically paved with golf balls.

When I got to the first tee, I reached for a driver. Even though it was now 1:45 in the afternoon and the green figured to be dried out, it would take incredible accuracy to hit the green and hold it. One of my luncheon companions had come along, and he looked as if there were nothing wrong with me that brain surgery couldn't cure. I addressed the ball as if it were my enemy, and hit it with everything I could get into it. The ball went up and hung in the sharp, clear air as if it had been painted there. When it came down—with overspin—it leaped forward right into the middle of the green.

Twenty feet from the hole.

Three hundred and forty-six yards and I'd not only driven the green but drilled it right in the heart!

Just like I'd been planning all along.

Two putts—birdie. I'd shown that my idea did work—that boldness could conquer this hole. And that if I made the first hole yield, then the whole course could be conquered with boldness. Suddenly my whole spirit, my entire attitude changed.

Arnold Palmer went on to birdie holes two, three and four. After a par at number five, he birdied the sixth and seventh holes. His score after nine was a remarkable 30. Palmer shot 35 on the inward half for 65, and victory.

Arnold's Darn Good Driving Technique

Palmer's swing has often been criticized because, aesthetically, it's not as nice as Sam Snead's. Granted, Palmer has always been a hitter of the golf ball rather than a swinger of a golf club. So he's not as smooth as Snead. Granted, too, he sort of loops the club in the finish, and that is anything but orthodox. But that's one of Palmer's trademarks. Besides, you shouldn't care what's done with the club after the ball has been struck. The truth is, all that really matters is that you arrive in a good impact position, with the sweet spot of the clubface spanking the dead center portion of the back of the ball. When Palmer was on the top of his game, he was there, baby, he was there. When it came to square contact, Palmer made that on the course as often as Mickey Mantle did on the baseball field.

One of the reasons Palmer is still a solid and accurate driver of the ball is a confident attitude. He stands on the tee, seeing a perfect drive come to life in his mind's eye before he even swings. For best results, mentally replay an earlier great tee shot that you hit.

The chief reason, however, for Palmer's great driving ability is his adherence to the fundamentals. Palmer has a fine grip. When you look at his hands on the club, you know instantly that they will work as a team. Both palms are parallel to one another, and he holds the club fairly lightly to encourage a smooth takeaway and a free releasing action through impact.

In setting up to the ball, Palmer drops his right foot back, farther from the target line than his left. This *closed* position allows him to swing the club along an inside path going back and on a more shallow path going through. Therefore, the club travels low to the ground and stays on the ball a split second longer. Ultimately, this means he will pick up added distance. Palmer keeps the club low to the ground in the takeaway and extends his hands well past his body at waist level before hinging his wrists. This promotes a solid weight shifting and turning action, plus a wide and powerful swing arc. When you pick up the club quickly and overhinge the wrists, the arc narrows and you lose distance.

At the top of the swing, Palmer keeps his right wrist relatively firm; this sets him up for a more powerful delayed hit. When you swing the club past parallel, the tendency is to overcock the right wrist. This fault, in turn, causes you to prematurely release the club—"cast"—and hit a high, weak slice. Therefore, like Arnie, you might want to employ a fairly compact swing—unless, of course, your John Daly-type backswing works wonders.

Palmer makes a solid weight shift to his left side on the downswing, then clears his left hip left of target, his right hip toward the target. Clearing the left hip gives him more freedom to deliver the club into the back of the ball. Rotating his right hip puts more oomph behind the hit.

Study the following photographs of Arnold Palmer's driver technique. Learning all twelve positions—from setup to impact—just may make you a more accurate tee-ball player.

The Arnold Palmer Swing: Position One

The Arnold Palmer Swing: Position Two

The Arnold Palmer Swing: Position Four

The Arnold Palmer Swing: Position Three

The Arnold Palmer Swing: Position Five

The Arnold Palmer Swing: Position Six

SuperGolf

The Arnold Palmer Swing: Position Seven

The Arnold Palmer Swing: Position Eight

The Arnold Palmer Swing: Position Nine

The Arnold Palmer Swing: Position Ten

SuperGolf

The Arnold Palmer Swing: Position Eleven

The Arnold Palmer Swing: Position Twelve

FUTURE FAMER: NICK FALDO

Nicholas Alexander Faldo was born July 18, 1957, in Welwyn Garden City, England. Faldo had a brief but impressive amateur career. After being a young international in 1974, he won the 1975 Berkshire Trophy, Scutton Jug, Hertfordshire Amateur, the County Champion of Champions, British Youths, Open Amateur Championship and the English Amateur Championship.

The 6'3" Faldo turned pro in 1976, at the young age of nineteen. That year he finished 58th on the European Tour's Order of Merit. It was obvious from the power he generated in his swing, and the superb touch he showed around the greens, that he would become a world beater one day soon. The following year he did not win a tournament, but he finished eighth on the Order of Merit. Furthermore, he made his Ryder Cup debut and finished with three victories in three matches, partnering Peter Oosterhuis to foursomes and fourballs wins. He also defeated British Open champion Tom Watson in the singles.

In 1978, he broke through, winning the Colgate PGA Championship. Faldo had a dry year in 1979, but 1980 to 1983 were fine years. In 1984, Faldo won the Car Care International on the European Tour and the Sea Pines Heritage Classic on the PGA Tour, proving he could compete with the Americans. However, he felt his swing wasn't good enough. He, like Hogan before him, searched for perfection. He asked renowned teacher David Leadbetter for advice. Leadbetter at the time just gave him some swing thoughts. They weren't good enough. Six months later, Faldo asked Leadbetter to help him overhaul his swing. Working on brand-new swing keys made 1985 and 1986 lean years, but the gamble and the hard work paid off.

In 1987, Faldo won the coveted British Open, his first major. Tour players must win major championships to be recognized as great golfers. In the years that followed, Faldo won five more majors: three Masters (1989, 1990 and 1996) and two British Opens (1990 and 1992). He also won many tournaments around the world, including the 1988 French Open and 1989 World Matchplay Championship. And his heroic defeat of Curtis Strange in the 1995 Ryder Cup helped his team to victory.

Faldo keeps his left foot planted to help promote a compact backswing.

Faldo, a full-time player on the PGA Tour, is now one of the game's most feared competitors. He works with a physical trainer and reports to Leadbetter for regular swing checkups at the Lake Nona Golf Club in Orlando, Florida, to keep both his body and his game in tip-top shape. Faldo is an all-around player, but his driving accuracy skills are exceptional. He has the most athletic on-balance swing of any player today, thanks to Leadbetter and Faldo's own hard work on the practice tee.

Faldo keeps his head behind the ball on the downswing to promote a solid upswing.

The key to Faldo's setup is placing 55 percent of his weight on his right foot and 45 on his left. Setting up with more weight on his right foot encourages him to make a solid weight shift into his right side. Amateurs tend to leave too much weight on their left foot during the backswing, then shift it over to their right on the downswing—one reason why their shots lack power.

On the backswing, Faldo keeps his left foot on the ground, and that helps him keep the action compact. The high handicap player allows his left foot to come well off the ground, causing him to lose the flex in his knees and the bend in his waist. This hinders his ability to coil, and that is another cause of lost power. This fault also causes you to swing the club on an overly steep backswing plane, then chop at the ball. Try leaving your left foot planted. You may find it helps sweep the ball off the tee.

The key to Faldo's downswing is keeping his head behind the ball, while shifting his weight and clearing his left hip. Keeping your head behind the ball will help you hit the ball more powerfully on the upswing.

You don't have to look into a crystal ball to know that Nick Faldo will win many more major championships. He has the game, the will, the concentration powers and the confidence to reach an even higher level of play. One would think, too, that eventually he will make it into the Hall of Fame.

5
WOODWORK

Hale Irwin is the master of hitting solid, super-controlled, soft-landing fairway wood shots.

Hale Irwin: the quiet man with a competitive fire of determination in his heart.

If one word could be used to sum up Hale Irwin's career, it would be *determination*. Irwin is a tenacious competitor who doesn't like to give up or get beaten. The harder the course—Harbour Town, Winged Foot, Butler National, Pinehurst, Inverness, Muirfield Village, Pebble Beach—the better Irwin plays. No wonder his fellow pros fear him.

Irwin's father taught him the game at an early age, forever emphasizing the importance of patience. He told Hale not to lose his head or get rattled when things didn't work out as planned, or to get overexcited by a great shot or score. The secret to playing a good game was keeping the emotions on an even keel. During the summers, most kids in Joplin, Missouri, spent their time swimming or riding bikes, not Irwin. His job was to head to the course early and work on his game. He'd practice on the range, play 18 holes, then practice some more. Irwin was always working hard on the fundamentals of the swing. To groove the correct grip, for example, he'd hit 300 practice balls, then spend a couple hours checking the positions of his palms and fingers in front of a mirror.

The Irwins moved to Boulder, Colorado, when Hale was 14, and there he was exposed to competition. From daylight to dark, Irwin and other junior golfers played matches against one another or had shotmaking contests among themselves. This is where he first learned to work the ball with a soft-fade flight. Unlike his friends, Irwin preferred practice to play. He figured there was little point in trying to shoot a low score if he didn't have a variety of shots in his bag. So he spent increasingly more time on the range perfecting his game.

Irwin's hard work and dedication to the sport paid off. The University of Colorado offered him a golf scholarship, and during his stay there, he won the NCAA Championship. A year later he turned pro.

As to be expected, Irwin found out that tour golf was much tougher than college golf. His swing had to stand up under intense pressure, and the putts had to drop. Par golf didn't win tournaments. By 1971, three years after turning pro, Irwin had become used to playing in the "heat" with the game's best players and rounded out any rough edges in his swing. That year, he won the 1971 Sea Pines Heritage Classic. Irwin must have loved that course because he won there again two years later. As excited as Irwin was about his success in the Heritage, nothing was sweeter than his first major championship win—the 1974 U.S. Open, played at the extremely difficult Winged Foot Golf Club in Mamaroneck, New York. That year, the United States Golf Association set up an extra-tough course, letting the rough grow long and making the greens very fast. As a result, the game's finest players shot high scores and became more and more frustrated as the championship competition continued. Even Jack Nicklaus and Tom Watson crumbled.

Not Hale Irwin. Taught to take the good with the bad by his father, Irwin thrived on difficult course conditions. Instead of taking risks off the tee, he played smart. Rather than attack the flag, he aimed for the "fat" or big portion of the green. He lagged putts, too, instead of charging the ball. Irwin's smart strategies earned him a spot in the winner's circle and a page in the history books.

Irwin won two more tournaments in 1975, two in 1976 and three in 1977. In 1979, Irwin won the U.S. Open at Inverness Country Club, a course famous for its lightning fast greens and tough pin placements. The confidence that Irwin had after his first Open win had a lot to do with his ability to perform so well against such golfing greats as Gary Player. Down the stretch, Irwin had a special intensity and confidence in his eyes. He also had such total control of his swing and short game that everyone watching him play knew he was destined to win.

After winning six more PGA Tour events between the years 1981 and 1985, Irwin added the final jewel to his U.S. Open crown, winning at Medinah in 1990. He won the championship in a playoff against Mike Donald, after scoring birdie on the 19th hole. Irwin looked somewhat stunned himself; I guess he never thought he'd be in a playoff. In the final round, he birdied holes 11, 12, 13 and 14. Then he sunk a 60-foot birdie putt on 18 to tie Donald. The funny thing about that putt was, once Irwin settled over the ball you had a feeling that he was going to make it. The look of determination was back in his eyes. Irwin was so excited about holing out that he ran around the 18th green high-fiving folks in the gallery. There wasn't a person within ten feet of Irwin that didn't get to give him skin. In the playoff, he set up yet another birdie by hitting a superb drive, then a seven-iron shot to within eight feet of the cup.

Hale Irwin proves that if you have the right amount of determination, you can accomplish just about anything in life. He also proves that you don't have to be a long driver of the ball to win golf tournaments. His success can be chalked up to his ability to hit pinpoint approaches with the fairway wood clubs.

There's one more chapter yet to be written in the Irwin story. He joined the Senior Tour in 1995. No doubt, if he keeps playing those on-target fairway wood shots, he'll win the Senior Open a few times before retiring. Let's see what his swing secrets are.

Hale's Hints for Good Fairway Wood Play

The most important element of Irwin's setup position involves ball position. When playing the fairway woods, Irwin plays the ball slightly forward of the center point in his stance. The average golfer misunderstands this principle. He plays the ball too far forward in his stance (off the left heel) and tries to sweep it off the turf. You'll want to take a slight divot, as does Irwin. So play the ball farther back in your stance than normal.

One key to Irwin's backswing is employing a full shoulder turn. Letting his left heel come slightly off the ground allows his shoulders and upper body to coil more powerfully. Many golfers are afraid of letting the left heel come off the ground, thinking that their body will shift laterally. However, if the left heel lifts up

A strong shoulder turn has always helped Irwin hit fairway wood shots more powerfully.

Hale's two chief downswing keys are shifting his weight to his left foot (top) and keeping his head back while his arms and hands release the club (bottom).

and the left knee moves "past" the ball, you'll make a more solid weight shift into your right side.

Another key to Irwin's good backswing position is to let the arms turn on a more upright plane than the shoulders. He keeps his arms in front of the body. If you swing the club too far inside the target line, you won't be able to nip the ball off tight fairway lies. On the downswing, Irwin shifts his weight solidly over to his left foot and leg. Replanting his left heel is the trigger he uses to set the downswing in motion. As his hips rotate counterclockwise and his hands and arms swing the club into the hitting area, Irwin keeps his head steady. Keeping the head behind the ball, while the lower body shifts toward the target and the hands, arms and club swing down, helps preserve your power until the precise moment of impact, when it's finally unleashed.

Because Irwin's arms and hands stay "soft" during the swing, they do a nice job of swinging around the body in the follow-through position. If there is tension or pressure in the arms and hands, you can't release the club correctly. To groove a solid weight shift action and free hands-arms release, practice this baseball drill that Irwin has used for over thirty years: With a fairway wood in your hands, stand with your feet together. Swing to the top. Step forward with your left foot. Swing through, allowing your hands, arms and right side to release toward an imaginary target.

FUTURE FAMER: COREY PAVIN

If you look up the word "competitor" in the dictionary, what you should find is a picture of Corey Pavin. This little man has hit some of the biggest shots in golf over the last few years. When the pressure is on and it's "white knuckle" time, Pavin becomes Superman. If you ever need someone to take on the school bully, Pavin's your man. If you need someone to hit a home run in the bottom of the ninth inning during the World Series, Pavin's your man. If you need someone to kick the winning field goal in the Super Bowl, with no time left on the clock, Pavin's your man. Of course, Pavin hasn't done all of these things yet, but what he has done is equally as impressive.

Pavin started playing golf when he was five years old, tagging along with his mom and dad on Southern California courses. He didn't show much true interest until the age of eight, when he started competing in local junior tournaments.

At the tender age of fifteen, Pavin began taking lessons from Bruce Hamilton, a local professional at the Los Posas Country Club. Hamilton encouraged Pavin to change his weak grip and to make some subtle changes in his setup and swing. Pavin listened to Hamilton, making the necessary changes to his technique. The lessons paid off. Within three months Pavin's handicap had dropped in half. But Pavin didn't sit on his laurels. He practiced harder than ever, and his high school senior year became a turning point in his career. He won the Catalina Open, breaking the tournament record. He won the Los Angeles men's championship (youngest winner ever). He won the Junior World Championship. That kind of play attracted golf coaches from colleges across the United States to Pavin.

Pavin finally decided to stay close to home and attend UCLA. Quickly adjusting to college life, his golf game took off. In his sophomore year, Pavin won six tournaments and was named first team All American. During his senior year, Pavin was on a roll, winning the PAC 10 Championship by seven strokes and five college tournaments.

Pavin next tried to qualify for the PGA Tour. He failed. After receiving feedback from friends and family, Pavin decided to play on the Asian Tour. Playing overseas and beating the likes of Greg Norman, Nick Faldo and Nick Price gave Pavin the confidence he needed to come back to the States and try the qualifying school again. The next time Pavin teed it up at the "Q" school, he was tournament tough, with a strong shotmaking game backing up a strong mental game. His drives were long and straight. His short game amazed everyone. His putter was on fire. Pavin had it all, as he proved by earning his PGA Tour card. He didn't act like a rookie, winning the Houston Open in 1984. Since that victory, Pavin has won a dozen more times. He was also the PGA Tour's leading money winner in 1991.

The most classic feature of Pavin's swing is his "cross-the-line" position at the top.

In 1995, Pavin's game moved up to the next level, a level where the names Nicklaus, Hogan and Watson are common. Pavin won the U.S. Open with a gutsy and determined performance at Shinnecock Hills Golf Club on Long Island. There, Pavin hit the shot that was heard around the golfing world. With golf's Great White Shark, Greg Norman, breathing down his neck, Pavin hit a fairway wood shot five feet from the hole on the 72nd hole to secure a par, and to win the championship.

In the fall of 1995, Pavin lead the American Ryder Cup team into Oak Hill to do battle with the European team. The highlight of the week for the American team was when Pavin chipped in for birdie to beat Nick Faldo and Bernhard Langer and put the Americans up on Saturday. Pavin's fairway wood shots, in which he sets his hands a little ahead of the ball, were remarkable as well.

The interesting point about Pavin's backswing is that, at the top, the club points to the right of the target. When the club's in this position, you can really "fire" your right side without worrying about coming over the top. Many great players have had the club point to the right at the top of the swing—Jack Nicklaus first comes to mind. Corey starts down with the hips clearing and the arms dropping to the inside practically simultaneously. At impact, the sweet spot of the clubface contacts the ball, owing to Pavin's consistently smooth rhythm and tempo.

Like Hale Irwin, Pavin never tries to overpower the ball. That's why the small man with the big heart will continue winning and one day fill a spot in golf's Hall of Fame.

6

LONG WAY "HOME"

Byron Nelson knows the secrets to cleanly sweeping long iron shots off the fairway.

Even today at age 84, Byron Nelson freely releases his right hand over his left: a swing key that enabled him to hit on-target long iron shots during his heyday.

When you think of Byron Nelson, you think of the eleven consecutive tournaments that he won, the eighteen wins in one single season, the lowest scoring average in the history of the Tour. Nelson was also the father of the modern golf swing. Nelson's swing was so good and pure that the United States Golf Association used it as the model for Iron Byron, a machine that tests golf balls and clubs.

Byron Nelson was born to John Byron Nelson and his wife, Madge Allen Nelson, on February 4, 1912, in Ellis County, on the outskirts of Waxahachie, Texas. If the size of a baby has anything to do with his destiny, John and Madge should have known that something big was going to happen to Byron; he weighed 12 pounds, 8 ounces.

Nelson was twelve years old when he noticed that some of his friends had extra nickels and dimes in their pockets. Curious where they got the extra money, he found out they all caddied at the Glen Garden Golf Course. The next weekend, Nelson showed up at the course, asking the caddie master for a job. There were sixty boys waiting to be caddies, so it took about five or six trips to the course before he got a bag. Nelson caddied whenever he could. He loved being outside in the fresh Texas air and thought that he had found the perfect job. After the golf season was over, Glen Garden held its annual party and golf tournament for the caddies. Even though Nelson had never played a round of golf, he decided to borrow a set of clubs and give the game a whirl. Nelson had a lot of fun that day, but he sure didn't give anyone a reason to believe that he would be a Hall of Famer. He shot 118, not counting the "whiffs."

Nelson saved up his caddying money and bought himself a mashie club, or a five iron by today's standards. He practiced whenever he had spare time. Once he had saved up some more money, he purchased a wood. Nelson learned how to play golf like a lot of the other boys—by watching good players swing. However, he learned more about the grip and correct alignment by reading Harry Vardon's book, *The Complete Golfer.*

Nelson kept caddying each summer until Ted Longworth, the head professional, asked Nelson if he would like to help out in the pro shop cleaning clubs, repairing old woods and buffing irons. Nelson became so good at repairing clubs that he made a set of irons that Ted used in the U.S. Open later that summer. Nelson worked hard in the pro shop, and hard on his game whenever he wasn't busy. He loved to practice and experiment with his swing, always trying new grips, address positions, backswings, trying to find a way to hit the ball better. As much as Nelson loved the long game, he realized at an early age that it didn't matter how much you practiced driving; if you couldn't chip and putt you weren't going to win. Nelson thus spent many long hours practicing chipping, pitching, putting and sand play.

The caddie tournament was held again at the end of the season, but it was only nine holes instead of eighteen. Nelson's game had so much improved, over only a short period of time, that he scored 40. Little did Nelson or the rest of the caddies know that the boy that Nelson tied—Ben Hogan—would become one of the greatest golfers of their generation. Nelson beat Hogan in a nine-hole playoff for the caddie championship. That wouldn't be the last time these two legends would square off against each another.

Nelson's game just kept getting better. He played in a few of the local junior tournaments and won more than his share. His great interest in playing golf made it awfully hard to concentrate on his school work. It was during the Depression, and Nelson thought that he could help out his family if he quit school and went to work. So halfway through his high school sophomore year he quit—a decision Nelson regretted the rest of his life.

In the summer of 1931, Nelson qualified for the U.S. Amateur in Chicago, but he had trouble putting on the bent grass greens. Being from Texas, he was used to Bermuda grass putting surfaces, which are a lot slower. Consequently, he failed to qualify for the match play segment of the tournament. That only made Nelson more determined. After reading about a tournament in Texarkana, which offered a total purse of $500, he decided to turn pro and hopped on a bus. Back then there was no Tour qualifying school. All you had to do was declare yourself a professional. Nelson played well and ended up with a third-place check of $75.

Back in the 1930s and 1940s, it was common for golf professionals to teach members during the summer and fall, then head west for the Winter Tour. That Tour started in California, headed to Texas and Florida and ended on the East coast in the spring. Nelson decided that this was his chance. He took off, planning to play in seven events. But his game wasn't as strong as it should have been, and he ran out of money after three events. Nelson returned to Texas, where he took on a club pro job making $60 a month. After the 1933 golf season, Nelson gave the Winter Tour another shot. With money he had borrowed from his future father-in-law and a car on loan from the local Ford dealer, Nelson had the backing to play in all the events, even if he got off to a bad start. That was not the case, however. Nelson got off to a great start and returned home with money enough to pay back his loans, get married and settle down.

In the spring of 1937, Nelson played in the Masters. He shot a course record 66 on Friday. But the turning point of the tournament was on Sunday, when leader Ralph Guldahl (the same person who beat Nelson badly in a junior tourney in Dallas years before) double bogeyed the 12th hole. Guldahl tried to make up ground on the 13th hole, where he gambled and lost yet another stroke to par. Nelson played the two holes a little differently, to say the least. On Number 12, Nelson hit a six iron to about six feet from the cup and made the putt for a birdie. On the 13th hole, a par five, Nelson went for the green in two shots, trying to make sure that he didn't push the ball into the water that guarded the right side of the green. He pulled the ball slightly left of the green, about twenty feet from the hole. He studied this shot closely, knowing that he had to hit the ball close. The shot was frightening because the green sloped away from Nelson. He had to be extra-careful not to hit the ball too hard and roll it through the green into Rae's Creek. After careful thought, Nelson elected to play a chip shot instead of a pitch. Did he ever make the right choice. He chipped the ball into the hole for an eagle three. Nelson had picked up six strokes on the leader in just two holes and was in the lead by three strokes.

Nelson continued his fine play, shooting 32 on the back nine. That score made Nelson realize that his game was as good as any other pro's on tour. It takes courage to be able to play that well on the last day of a major championship, and Nelson passed the test with flying colors. He won the Masters by two strokes. (In 1958, Augusta National commemorated the bridge on numbers 12 and 13 to the spectacular play of Byron Nelson on that sunny day twenty-one years earlier.)

In 1939, Nelson moved up the ladder farther, capturing the U.S. Open at age 27. Many golfers remember this Open because Sam Snead bogeyed the 17th hole and triple-bogeyed the 18th hole to miss a 36-hole playoff by one stroke. Nelson won that playoff, and the title, by beating Craig Wood. But the dramatics happened before the playoff. Nelson played like a golfer who was possessed, hitting the flagstick six times—with a one iron, four iron, five iron, six iron, a wedge and, of all clubs, a driver!

Nelson won the 1942 Masters, beating his old caddie friend

Ben Hogan in an 18-hole playoff. In 1944, Nelson won thirteen of the twenty-three events he played in and won a record $37,967.69. In 1945, at age 33, Nelson won eighteen of the tour's thirty-five tournaments, including a string of eleven tournaments in a row. From mid-March to early August, he finished first every single time. (Nancy Lopez won five times in a row in 1978, the closest any other golfer has come to this record.) Nelson's scoring average for the year was an incredible 68.33—a record that will probably never be broken. The closest that anyone has come to it was Greg Norman in 1994 with 68.81. Nelson was never able to explain or understand what happened to him that summer of 1945. It seemed like he had complete control of the ball—in the air and on the ground.

After losing in a three-way playoff for the U.S. Open of 1946 (his caddie stepped on his ball during the final round, causing Nelson to take a one-stroke penalty), he quit playing tournament golf, bought a 700-acre farm and retired to Texas to become a farmer.

Byron Nelson was truly in command of his total game. But it was his long-iron play that set him apart. Nelson was more accurate with a one iron or two iron than most of his contemporaries were with a five iron. Until Nelson came along, most players swung the club on a flat plane, using exaggerated hand and wrist action to produce low running shots. Nelson discovered that if he took the club straight back in a line away from the ball, then used a lateral shift with the lower body on the downswing, he could keep the club moving down the target line longer and hit a straighter shot. Nelson was credited with being the father of the modern swing.

When young Nelson was perfecting his craft, golf equipment was in a transitional period. Clubs had previously been made with wooden shafts, primarily flexible ones of hickory. Nelson had developed a flat caddie swing, requiring a lot of hand and wrist action on the backswing and downswing—and perfect timing—to square the clubface at impact. In the 1930s, clubs were making the change from wooden shafts to steel. Steel shafts were much stiffer than those made of hickory, so with his flat caddie swing, Nelson hooked the ball. He discovered that, with the firmer shaft, he didn't need to be quite so "handsy." Once Nelson quieted down his hands, his shots became more accurate. Let's see why Iron Byron became such a master of the long irons.

Long Iron Lessons from "Lord Nelson"

Nelson believed that the proper setup and takeaway were critical to hitting the long irons far and straight. Nelson's posture was a little different from most players of his generation. He stood close to the ball. As a tall man, it appeared as though he was crowding the ball. But he didn't; he stood just close enough to the ball for the arms to hang and extend naturally. He bent over from his hips, so that the club's angle matched the angle of his spine. When you crowd the ball, and stoop over, the arms bend at the elbow and you lose the ability to turn and rotate your body.

Nelson placed his feet slightly wider apart than his shoulders. This seemingly incidental characteristic of the setup will help you make an extended takeaway and swing the club on a wide arc. To promote solid contact at impact, he played the ball about three inches inside of the left heel. Once Nelson settled into this address position, he turned his head to look at the target. This helped him align the clubface and his body square to the target.

Nelson thought that it was imperative to set the sweet spot of the clubface directly behind the ball. Some pros play the ball off the club's heel or toe end. That's because they are allowing or adjusting for some idiosyncratic swing action. Set the club down squarely behind the ball at address and the club is likely to finish square to the ball at impact. Nelson knew that if he swung the club back on the correct square arc, he could return the club squarely to the ball at impact, without making any compensations during the swing. Therefore, one secret to Nelson's mastery of the long irons was taking the club straight back along the target line for about fourteen inches.

The distance that you swing the club back is in direct relationship to how flexible and supple you are in your upper body. Nelson never tried to swing back too far. He was in total control of his backswing, only swinging back as far as his turning shoulders and arm swing took him. As he swung the club to the top, his left arm remained relatively straight—never stiff. The swinging weight of the clubhead allowed his wrists to hinge. Many golfers think they have to consciously cock their wrists once they complete their takeaway. Don't. Let them hinge naturally as you swing the club to the top.

Nelson made the smoothest transition from backswing to downswing of any player of his era. His downswing worked as a perfect chain reaction: feet first, then knees, hips, shoulders, arms, hands, club. Your downswing will operate on automatic pilot, too, if you trigger the action by making a solid weight shift from the right foot to the left. Another interesting thing about Nelson's downswing was that he appeared to dip or "become shorter." The reason: He kept his knees flexed and moving laterally longer than most players. This helped him swing down a more shallow path and sweep the ball solidly off grass or a tee. Amateur golfers have a tendency to come out of their shots because they straighten their left knee before impact. This prevents a solid weight shift and turning action of the body through the ball, resulting in a topped shot.

A perfect example of Nelson hitting his long irons right on the button was in the Durham Open of 1945. Nelson had just started his streak, winning three tournaments in a row. The competitors played 36 holes on the final day, and Nelson was trailing Tony Penna by a few strokes in the morning round. The 18th hole at Hope Valley was a par three of 210 yards. Nelson took out his one iron and hit the shot perfectly to within four feet of the hole. After careful thought, Nelson made the putt.

In the afternoon round, Nelson came to 18 trailing Penna by one stroke. Again, Nelson took out his one iron and hit a high fade that came to rest fifteen feet from the cup. Nelson looked the putt over from all angles, knowing that he had to hole it to force a playoff and keep the streak alive. The ball broke about a foot and fell into the hole. He had played the hole twice in a total of four strokes. Nelson went on to win the playoff and keep the streak alive.

Even today, at 84, Byron Nelson can still play the long irons well. That's because he sets up square to the target, makes a solid backswing and, most of all, freely releases his right hand and arm over his left hand and arm. If you do this, the toe of the club will lead the heel through impact, giving you the draw flight you dream about.

FUTURE FAMER: BERNHARD LANGER

Germany's Bernhard Langer has golf talent, total dedication, a winning attitude, an excellent tournament track record and the ability to concentrate for five straight hours when competing against the best players in the world. Since Hogan, nobody focuses on the shot at hand and stays in the moment better than

Langer. For these reasons and more, he will one day be a Hall of Fame member. Langer is also a perfectionist who leaves nothing to chance. For example, he has been known to take a yardage wheel out to the course during practice rounds to check distances. Why? He abhors hitting the wrong club even once during a championship. You've gotta beat Langer. He doesn't beat himself.

Bernhard Langer is golf's current long iron wizard.

Bernhard Langer was born in Auhausen, West Germany, in 1957. Officially, he was hired as a caddie at the Augsburg Golf Course, but the club had so few members that much of Langer's time was spent practicing on the driving range. As a youngster, Langer was small in size, so he wasn't able to hit the ball very far. Ironically, this worked in his favor. Because he didn't hit the ball long off the tee, he had to play a lot of long irons into greens, an explanation for why he is considered the best long iron player in the game today.

Most fifteen-year-old boys dream about getting a driver's license or meeting the perfect girl. Not Langer. He decided to quit school and turn professional. This decision shocked his parents because at the time golf was a minor sport in Germany—so minor that there were only a few courses in the entire country—and the possibility of Langer making it as a pro seemed a long shot.

At first Langer struggled on Tour. He broke through in 1979 to win the Cacharel Under–25 Championship by the biggest margin ever—17 strokes. Langer was now confident that he had "it." The German's next gigantic win came in 1985 when he won the Masters. Langer dazzled the crowds at Augusta with his brilliant shotmaking and deft putting stroke. Langer became the first German to win the green jacket and only the third foreign player to win at Augusta. Langer kept up his brilliant play, winning the Sea Pines Heritage Classic the following year. Not only did Langer play well in the United States, he racked up victories in Europe as well, adding the German Open and the European Open to his collection of trophies. His winning streak continues.

The strongest part of Langer's game is the long irons. Like Byron Nelson before him, he feels more comfortable with a two or three iron in his hand than a middle or short iron. Langer is able to control these clubs because of his beautiful tempo. He never swings fast, which is the secret to hitting the long irons. Bernard's setup is classic. He puts himself in a position to make a good swing before the club starts back by having his left arm and clubshaft form a straight line. He knows that as long as he swings this longer radius (and doesn't let the left arm bend dramatically during the swing), he'll hit powerfully accurate shots.

The chief positive element of Langer's backswing is his body coil. Boy, does he wind up! Here's a perfect example of how Langer's powerful coil helped him: In the final round of the 1993 Masters, Langer had a two-stroke lead over Chip Beck. On the 13th hole, a tough par five where Masters have been won and lost many times, Langer hit his tee shot close to trees that border the left side of the fairway. Langer took his time and calculated the distance to be 205 yards to the center of the green for his second shot. He knew that this shot had to be hit perfectly. If he hit the ball a little off center it wouldn't carry over Rae's Creek, which guards the front portion of the green. Langer decided on his favorite club, the three iron, to determine his fate. He couldn't have made a better choice. Langer moved the ball back in his stance, a little more to the center of his body, which would help him hit down and impart backspin. Then, he made a 100-degree shoulder turn and swung down powerfully. The second Langer hit the shot he knew it was a good one; he just didn't realize at the time how good a shot it was. The ball stopped just twenty feet from the pin. After surveying the putt, Langer rolled it right into the center of the cup, for an eagle three. Langer had mounted a charge that reminded the gallery of the days when Arnold Palmer hitched up his pants before hitting one of his familiar miracle shots at Augusta National. Langer made one more birdie coming in and won his second green jacket.

Langer's strong shoulder turn is not the only reason he hits such powerful long iron shots. He pulls the club down into the hitting area with the back of his left hand facing the target. This one key allows him to put the sweet spot of the clubface on the ball practically every time.

Try Langer's swing tips. They may not make you a future Hall of Famer, but they'll lower your scores and brighten your golfing future.

7

THE IRON MAN

Precise middle iron and short iron play made
Lee Trevino a legend in his own time.

Lee Trevino: "The Merry Mex"

The game of golf owes great thanks to Lee Buck Trevino, whose heartwarming, rags to riches story would have made Cecil B. DeMille stand on his head. It's true Hollywood stuff. Trevino rejuvenated the game in the late 1960s, when golfers were looking for a new breed of hero to embrace. Jack Nicklaus beat golfing icon Arnold Palmer in the 1962 U.S. Open, and Arnie's Army didn't like that. Galleries wanted someone they could call their own. Lee Trevino fit the bill. He had anything but a classic swing; he cracked jokes and chattered between shots. Trevino made the somewhat stodgy sport of golf seem less grim. He made it fun.

There was a braggart quality about the young "Merry Mex." But he backed up his big words with superb shotmaking, particularly in the departments of short iron and middle iron play. Club level golfers loved watching the guy from the other side of the tracks beat the Tour's seasoned big guns. There will never be another Lee Trevino. He truly is one of a kind.

Trevino was born December 1, 1939, in Dallas, Texas. His mother was Juanita Trevino. He didn't know who his father was. Raised by his grandparents in a tiny two-room shack on the outskirts of Dallas, the poverty-stricken Trevino made up his mind at an early age to succeed—his own way. School didn't appeal much to him, so he headed off and joined the Marines at the age of 17. Although Trevino had tried golf before, in the service he had the time and money to work on his game. He played on the Marines golf team, often traveling to Japan, the Philippines and other exotic destinations to compete. Trevino was getting his education on the road. His team won all their matches. Personally, though, he thought he was the best player in the armed forces, until Sergeant Orville Moody, a big Okie, beat him by 19 strokes.

In 1960, shortly after being discharged, Trevino took a job at Hardy's driving range in Dallas. There he further honed his shotmaking skills, hitting hundreds of balls a day. When not at the range, he could usually be found gambling on the Tenison Park course. As Trevino once said, "True pressure is playing a $5 Nassau with $1 in your pocket."

Trevino won a number of local PGA tournaments, but he wasn't sure he was ready for the Tour. In 1967, he would find out how ready he was. He led the nation in the local qualifying for the U.S. Open, shooting 134 for 36 holes. Next up was sectional qualifying in Dallas. Trevino kept up his hot streak, finishing second and earning an entry into the Open, which was being played that year at Baltusrol in New Jersey. He played well enough to finish fifth and earned the most money he had ever seen at one time—$6,000. That check, and a top ten finish at Baltusrol, would be a harbinger of what was to come.

In 1968, the Apollo spacecraft circled the moon ten times, drug use reached an all-time high and riots at the Chicago Democratic Convention stunned the nation. The most shocking news on the golf front, however, was that a virtually unknown Mexican-American had come out of nowhere to win the U.S. Open. Trevino fired a final round score of 69 to beat Jack Nicklaus by four strokes at Oak Hill Country Club in Rochester, New York. Trevino's total of 275 tied the Open record that Nicklaus had set the year before. Trevino also shot four rounds in the 60s, a first in the history of the Open. With a first-place check of $30,000 in his pocket and all the confidence in the world, Trevino was off and running. He won the Hawaiian Open later that year and several other tournaments over the next couple of Tour seasons.

In 1971, Trevino started a torrid winning streak that would rival Byron Nelson's. Trevino won his second U.S. Open title, beating Jack Nicklaus in a playoff at the famed Merion course in Pennsylvania. The playoff started off on a humorous note. While searching in his golf bag for a new glove, Trevino found a rubber snake that belonged to his daughter Leslie. Trevino pulled the snake out, then tossed it over near Nicklaus. Since Jack had his back to Trevino he didn't know the snake was fake. When he saw it in the grass, he jumped about three feet in the air. A bit of gamesmanship on Trevino's part? We'll never know. What we do know is that Trevino won the playoff, 68 to 71.

The next big tournament that Trevino won was the Canadian Open, in a playoff with Art Wall. It was on to the British Open, being played at Royal Birkdale. Trevino had played Birkdale in the 1969 Ryder Cup matches, so he was familiar with the course. With his confidence sky-high, Trevino knew this was going to be his Open. Of all the kinds of courses that Trevino played on, the British-style links fit his game better than any other. Trevino was an expert at playing the bump-and-run shot. Also, having grown up in windy Texas, he knew how to handle the ocean breeze that blew hard that year at Birkdale. Trevino shot 278 to win his third national title in just twenty days. Another British Open victory followed in 1972, at Muirfield in Scotland, when Trevino beat Nicklaus by one stroke. "Super Mex" loved to beat the "Golden Bear." Nicklaus was the greatest golfer that ever lived, so any time Trevino was in the hunt with Nicklaus, he psyched himself up and took his game to a higher level.

Trevino won the 1974 PGA Championship over Jack Nicklaus at the Tanglewood Golf Course in Winston-Salem, North Carolina. Trevino shot 276, and it looked as though no golfer would ever beat him again. Trevino was the most popular player in golf, too. People enjoyed watching him hit a perfectly controlled fade, off the tee and on approach shots. They also loved listening to Trevino's one-liners. It didn't matter whether it was the final round of the U.S. Open or the Wednesday Pro-Am, Trevino enjoyed joking around with the gallery—until it was time to play a shot. Then, and only then, Trevino was all business.

In 1975, at the Western Open, it took an act from the heavens to slow down Lee Trevino. Play had been suspended for rain. Trevino was leaning up against his golf bag when a thunderous crack sounded. A split second later, Trevino was lifted a foot into the air, then dropped to the ground by lightning. The lightning had traveled through the metal shafts of his golf clubs and out through his back. Trevino was rushed to the hospital, where he remained in intensive care for two full days. Off and on, from that day onward, Trevino has suffered severe back problems. One more stroke of misfortune concerned a bad business deal that left Trevino losing much of the money he had won around the world. Nevertheless, Trevino proved that you can't keep a true champion down.

In 1984, Trevino won his second PGA Championship, at Shoal Creek in Birmingham, Alabama. He would go on to dominate the Senior PGA Tour a few years later, winning over twenty-five titles and leading the Seniors' money list twice. This accomplishment goes well with his twenty-seven PGA Tour titles. Trevino's still winning on the Senior PGA Tour, and probably will for years to come.

Lee Trevino is the last of a dying breed of feel players, who learned golf by instinct. Trevino is a self-taught player who never took a lesson, because in his words, "I never found a teacher who could beat me." He thinks today's PGA Tour pros rely too much on coaches and are far too technically minded. That explains why so many naturally talented young golfers suffer from "paralysis by analysis" and lose their PGA Tour cards after spending only a couple of years playing the tournament circuit.

When Trevino plays, his medium and short iron shots seem to be guided by radar. Case in point: the 1987 Skins Game played at the beautiful but difficult PGA West course in Palm Springs, California. Playing the 17th hole, a diabolical par three of 167 yards nicknamed "Alcatraz," Trevino faced a shot to an island green. There was a slight breeze that crisp fall day, so Trevino knew he had to hit a solid six iron to reach the hole. Trevino settled into his unique setup position, then swung. As soon as the ball took off, he knew it was a good shot. The ball started flying left of the target, drifted back to the right, landed on the green, took two bounces, then rolled into the center of the cup. Hole in one! The shot earned Trevino $175,000 in "skins" money. To prove that it wasn't a fluke, on the very next hole Trevino used the six iron again and hit the ball close for another skin. These two six-iron shots earned Trevino $310,000.

Trevino's Texas-Bred Iron Technique

One thing that catches your eye when you watch Lee Trevino's setup is the position of his feet. He uses an extra-wide stance because that gives him a strong platform, or foundation, to swing from. He has always believed that it's difficult to employ fluid lower body action if the feet are close together. Trevino also fans his left foot well outward and sets his right foot perpendicular to the target line. His right-foot position prevents him from swaying his body on the backswing. His left-foot position helps him clear his hips left of the target on the downswing, opening a clear passageway for the hands and arms to deliver the clubface solidly into the ball.

Another thing that's unique about Trevino's address is that he plays the ball back in the stance. This position allows him to hit the ball low and explains why he has done so well on windy British links courses. Playing the ball back also allows Trevino to impart backspin on the ball—an advantage on firm greens. It also lets you to hit the ball over a hazard, well past the pin, then spin it back to the hole.

SuperGolf

When setting up to play a short or medium iron shot, Trevino assumes an extra-wide stance and plays the ball well back in it.

Trevino's unique takeaway swing technique; he fans open the clubface.

Trevino is halfway back and his hips still have not rotated.

Even though Trevino employs a compact swing, he still makes a strong body turn.

SuperGolf

Notice Trevino's vigorous weight-shifting and hip-clearing actions.

Notice how the left arm pulls the club into the "slot."

Trevino's strong leg-drive action keeps the club heading for the back of the ball.

Trevino's vigorous hip-clearing action helps him drive the club powerfully into the ball.

Trevino swings the club back outside the target line because he learned through trial and error that this path sets him up to hit a super-controlled left-to-right fade shot. As Trevino pushes the club outside the target line with his left hand and arm, his hips and shoulders roll. His backswing is compact but powerful and very controlled.

As Trevino starts the downswing, his hips rotate quickly to the left, while his arms swing the club outward, toward the ball. Some teachers have commented that it looks like Trevino's hips rotate toward third base, while his arms swing to first base. He's a classic left-sided player. Many amateur golfers who come over the top on the downswing and hit a pull slice can learn a lot from watching Trevino's lower body action. He triggers the downswing by shifting his hips laterally, then rotates them to the left quickly. When you do that, you can't come over the top.

Once Trevino's weight shifts to his left foot, he pulls the club down with his left hand and arm, then hits against a firm left side.

FUTURE FAMER: TOM KITE

No wonder the press call Tom Kite "Tom Terrific." He stands only 5'8" and weighs 150 pounds, yet he's a master shotmaker, with over 9 million dollars in the bank and a U.S. Open trophy resting on his living room mantel. If you ever read the story about the little engine that could, you will agree it certainly applies to Tom Kite. What Kite lacks in size, he makes up through hard work and determination. Since Ben Hogan, no pro golfer has worked harder on his game. Kite has probably taken more lessons from different teaching professionals than any player on the PGA Tour. His philosophy: If you aren't learning and improving every day, you're losing ground.

Kite started playing golf with his father at the age of six in Dallas, Texas. By the time he was eleven, he was already shooting in the 70s. But when the family moved to Austin, Kite's game really took off, owing to lessons from the late Harvey Penick, the golf professional at the Austin Country Club.

Tom Kite's hard practice helps him play to a high standard.

Kite attended the University of Texas, where he was an All American. In 1970, he was runner up to Lanny Wadkins in the United States Amateur Championship. Two years later he tied fellow teammate Ben Crenshaw for the NCAA Individual Championship. Kite's performance in these two premier amateur events prompted him to turn professional in 1972. Kite won for the first time in 1976, capturing the IVB-Bicentennial Golf Classic. After that victory, he played with the dogged determination of a gunfighter looking to add notches to his trusty pistol.

By 1992, Kite had done just about everything there is to do in professional golf. He had been the PGA Tour's leading money winner. He had been a member of the Ryder Cup team seven times. He'd won fifteen tournaments. But the one thing that Kite wanted most—a victory in a major championship—had eluded him. In June 1992, life for Tom Kite took a new turn when he captured the U.S. Open. Some say the victory was due to his accurate driving. Others think it was his chip-in on hole number 7 on day four. Others, still, say it was his putting. The experts, however, know that Kite's victory can be attributed most to the superb medium and short iron shots he played on many of the 72 holes.

Kite's technique is fundamentally very sound. He uses a neutral grip, meaning that the "V"s formed by the thumb and forefinger of each hand point midway between his chin and right shoulder. This grip unifies the hands, thereby preventing one hand from taking control.

Kite turns his shoulders twice as far as his hips on the backswing and makes a solid weight shift into his right side. Like Trevino, his backswing is compact. As he shifts his weight to his left side on the downswing, the club drops down on a slightly flatter plane, allowing him to sweep the ball off the turf. This sweeping action prevents dirt from intervening between the ball and clubface at impact. When this happens, the ball flies uncontrollably off the clubface, sometimes as much as 20 yards farther than normal. Kite's contact is clean, and that explains why his distance control is so consistent.

Another reason Kite's iron shots fly on target the correct distance is because he regularly grooves a square alignment posi-

To groove a square setup, Kite hits balls with two clubs parallel to the target line.

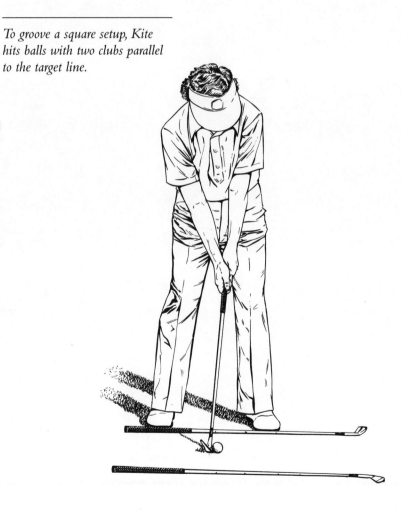

tion—by hitting practice balls with one club lying on the ground parallel to the target line, another across his feet.

You may not play like Tom Kite if you adopt the same practice ethic. You will, however, hit better medium and short iron shots, and probably lower your scores in the process.

8

HOUDINI IS ALIVE

When it comes to recovering from trouble spots off the fairway, no player can touch Seve Ballesteros.

Seve Ballesteros, golf's all-time trouble-play virtuoso.

Severiano Ballesteros was born on April 9, 1957, in Pedrena, a sleepy small town in the northern part of Spain. Seve, a farmer's son, came up the hard way. He learned golf and became famous the old-fashioned way: *He earned it.*

Ballesteros was the nephew of the great golfer Ramon Sota. But while growing up, Seve had no formal training. His parents weren't thrilled about his taking golf so seriously. That was probably the reason Sota didn't give him lessons. Golf was a rich man's sport, too. Juniors of non-golfing parents were not allowed to play the local courses. Caddies weren't allowed to play either. Instead of letting this get him down, Ballesteros practiced with the trusty three iron his older brother, Manuel, had given him when he was eight. After this club was stolen, he practiced with a five iron. Sometimes he sneaked onto the Pedrena course to practice. Most often, he hit shots in the caddie yard, on the beach or in the fields behind his family's farmhouse where he had constructed a course consisting of two holes: one 100 yards long, the other 180 yards. The course wasn't manicured. Ironically, having to hit shots out of bad lies trained Ballesteros to become a more versatile trouble player.

Practicing with one club taught Ballesteros this: Working the body in different ways and swinging the club on different paths and planes—with the face open, closed or square—produces various shots. This kind of practice also forces you to use your imagination and concentrate more intently.

Early on, Ballesteros actually found the challenge of planning and playing a recovery shot with one club as exciting as trying to hit the ball long. He would hit shots with the ball in the middle of his stance, off his left heel, close to his right heel. One time he'd put his weight on his left foot, another time on his right. He opened the clubface, closed the clubface. He took the club back outside the target line, then cut across it going through. Other times he'd take the club back well inside the target line, then let the toe of the clubhead lead its heel through impact. He'd allow his head to move on the backswing, then keep it steady on the next swing. He used light grip pressure, firm grip pressure. He tried dead-handed shots and handsy shots. He tried different combinations of setup positions. For example, one time he would play the ball back, keep most of his weight on his left foot and swing on an upright plane; another time, he would play the ball forward, setup with slightly more weight on his right foot and swing on a flat plane.

Ballesteros was a grand experimenter. Each time he hit a shot from a different lie with a different swing, he'd make a mental note of how the ball reacted in the air and on the ground. The more swings he developed, the more imaginative he became. The more his imagination grew, the more versatile his shotmaking skills turned out to be.

A great shot woke the golf world to Ballesteros' shotmaking prowess. He hit it at Royal Birkdale during the 1976 British Open. On the final hole, his second shot finished 25 yards to the left of the green, pin high. There had been a drought in England, so the green was baked out from the sun and exceptionally fast. The ball sat on virtual hardpan. Two bunkers guarded the green. The wind was at Ballesteros' back. The circumstances did not allow him to hit a high pitch shot. The ball had no cushion under it, making it difficult to loft it softly into the air. Besides, the green was too firm to hold the ball. Inevitably, the ball would land on the green and bounce into more trouble. That, however, seemed the only shot—to everyone but Ballesteros. He played the most delicate pitch-and-run shot, which landed on a narrow dirt path between the bunkers, bounced once, rolled toward the pin and came to rest four feet from the hole.

Ballesteros made the tap-in birdie to finish second to Jack Nicklaus—at 19 years old.

Because he was so young, and seemingly inexperienced, golf writers deemed Ballesteros a shotmaking genius. He quickly pointed out to the press that he had learned his skill with one club and had been hitting shots like this for eleven years.

Ballesteros, who had turned pro in 1974, finished first on the European Tour's Order of Merit the same year he hit the great shot at Birkdale. From 1977 to 1979, Ballesteros would stay at the top. During this time frame, he won several big tournaments, including the Lancome Trophy, the English Golf Classic and the German, Scandinavian and Swiss opens. He also won the Greater Greensboro Open in the United States. No win, however, was bigger than his 1979 British Open victory—Ballesteros' first major championship. It was obvious to many who watched that this wouldn't be his last, and those who predicted Ballesteros would make it big were right. In 1980, he captured his second major title, the Masters.

The highlight of Ballesteros' 1981 season on the European Tour was his win in the Suntory World Matchplay Championship. A year later, he flew back to Spain with a second green jacket, after again winning the Masters. He also won the Westchester Classic. In 1983, he finished second on the Order of Merit, owing to victories in the Sun Alliance PGA Championship, Carrolls Irish Open and the Lancome Trophy. The next year, 1984, was also big for him. He won his second British Open and second Suntory World Matchplay. He had another fine year in 1985, finishing third on the European Tour's Order of Merit. He also won the USF&G Classic in America. In 1986, the sensational Spaniard returned to the top spot on the European Tour after winning six events.

In 1987, his only win was the Suze Open, but he returned to

form the following year, winning the British Open for the third time and finishing top of the Order of Merit. He also managed to win the Westchester Classic in the United States. The next time he finished first on the Order of Merit was in 1991. In 1992 and 1993, he fell into a slump. Many golf experts think his driving problems were caused by his seeking out instruction from the game's teaching gurus, including David Leadbetter and Mac O'Grady. The consensus: Ballesteros should have stayed a natural golfer. In 1994, he bounced back, winning two tournaments and finishing third on the Order of Merit.

In 1995 his driving problems caused him to lay off golf for six months. He has since returned to the game and, of course, has his eye on winning major championships. Many doubt he will make a comeback, but Ballesteros loves being the underdog. So look out, PGA Tour pros. He has nothing to prove, and if his driving game is half as good as it used to be, he can still win on tour because of his exceptional trouble-play game.

Seve's Sensational Trouble-Play Skills

Some of the trouble shots that Ballesteros has hit over the years to win over 60 tournaments and to play so well in eight Ryder Cup matches are the short punch, the greenside shot from side-hill lie (ball below feet), the short iron out of thick rough, the cut shot off an uphill bank and the downhill chip from light rough. These quick tips should help you play these shots like Ballesteros.

THE SHORT PUNCH Put 65 percent of your weight on your left foot. Make a firm-wristed, compact swing. In swinging down, let your hands lead the club.

In playing a short punch shot, back to the fairway, Ballesteros lets his hands lead the club into the ball.

THE SIDEHILL SHOT (BALL BELOW FEET) Aim your feet, knees, hips and shoulders—and the clubface—left of target to compensate for the ball fading from left to right in the air. Bend more at the waist and knees, then maintain that added flex on the back and forward swings.

THE IRON FROM THICK ROUGH Set up with 60 percent of your weight on your left foot. Swing the club on a very steep plane, letting your wrists hinge. Allow your left hip to clear, then pull the club down hard into the back of the ball.

SuperGolf

Aim your body left, as Ballesteros does here, when hitting a ball that's below your feet.

When playing an iron shot from thick rough, Ballesteros pulls the club down hard with his hands and arms.

THE CUT SHOT OFF AN UPHILL LIE Set up with the clubface open. Swing the club back outside the target line. Swing across the ball on the downswing, holding onto the club more tightly with your left hand. Keep your head behind the ball to encourage an upswing hit. In the hitting area, try to point the face of the club toward the sky.

THE DOWNHILL CHIP FROM LIGHT ROUGH Put 70 percent of your weight on your left foot. Lay the face of a third wedge wide

To hit a short cut shot off an uphill lie, swing across the ball on the downswing, as Ballesteros does here.

open to compensate for the clubface closing at impact. Play the ball back, about six inches behind your left heel. Set your hands well ahead of the ball. Make a one-piece takeaway, swinging the club back together with your hands, arms and shoulders. Swing the club down the slope.

In setting up to play a downhill chip, Ballesteros puts seventy percent of his weight on his left foot.

FUTURE FAMER: FRED COUPLES

Frederick Stephen Couples was born October 3, 1959, in Seattle, Washington. Couples was fortunate to have been blessed with the same strong, quick hands that made his father a star semipro baseball player. Ironically, his father didn't want him to become a pro golfer; neither did his mother. They knew how difficult it was to make it in pro sports. Like so many parents, they wanted him to "be somebody," a lawyer or doctor, for example.

Couples got into golf at the age of eleven, when his brother's best friend gave him a set of used clubs. Couples taught himself the game. After riding his bicycle to Jefferson Park, a nine-hole course in his hometown, he'd usually go around twice. By the time he was thirteen, he could hit the ball fairly accurately and powerfully. He started playing with older locals, wagering a little to get a feel for playing under pressure.

Later Couples played in Catholic high school, then for the University of Houston team. College golf helped Couples evolve as a player, although he remained self-taught. In 1978, he was named All American and won both the Washington State Amateur and Open titles. That same year he finished low amateur in the U.S. Open at Cherry Hills Golf Club in Denver, Colorado.

Couples turned pro in late 1980, but he didn't actually start competing until 1981. That year he won $78,939, more than any other rookie, and finished 53rd on the PGA Tour money list. The following year Couples finished 53rd again. In 1983, he broke through to win his first tournament, the Kemper Open. He moved to 19th on the money list, causing the golf world to take notice. By 1984, Couples was hitting the ball longer than ever, and his short game had improved dramatically. That's why he won the Tournament Players Championship and finished seventh on the money list with $334,573. Couples has definitely become "somebody."

From 1985 to 1991, Couples won four more times. In 1987, he started taking lessons from Paul Marchand at the Houston Country Club and has been going for regular swing tune-ups ever since. In 1992, Couples reached a new level, winning the

Even on days when his driving game is off, Fred Couples manages to shoot low scores because of his trouble-play expertise.

coveted Masters title, his first major. He finished first on the money list that year, thanks to wins at the Los Angeles Open and Nestle Invitational. Couples had good years in 1993 and 1994, but in 1995, he didn't play so well, owing to back problems. In 1996, he proved he was back by winning the Tournament Players Championship.

Throughout Couples' career, he has been known as one of the most powerful hitters on tour. He misses the fairway around 40 percent of the time, but thanks to some great recovery shots, he manages to hit a high number of greens in regulation and shoot low scores. Take 1994, for example. Couples was ranked 172 in driving accuracy. Yet he ranked 12th in greens hit in regulation and second in scoring, with a 69.28 average. Look for Couples to hit great recovery shots for a long time to come, like the 252-yard two-iron shot he hit from light rough on the par-five final hole of the 1993 World Cup played at the Lake Nona Golf Club in Orlando, Florida. Couples holed out, for an eagle two, enabling him and partner Davis Love to go on to win the event.

Here's how to hit a powerful long iron from light rough. Approach this shot with confidence. Today's long irons have a more generous sweet spot and are more sole-weighted, so it's easier to loft the ball into the air. When setting up, play the ball slightly back in your stance; this address position promotes a narrower swing plane and cleaner clubface-to-ball contact. Keep the backswing compact, since a long swing can cause you to lose your balance. On the downswing, keep your head behind the ball as weight shifts to your left foot and your left hip clears. To ensure that you hit through the ball, imagine there is a second ball a couple of inches in front of the one you're actually going to hit. Trying to hit that imaginary ball will allow you to make more solid contact.

When Couples played this shot at the World Cup, the rough grass was short, not lush. In fact, it was kind of dry. That's one reason the long iron plowed through the grass so easily. Don't try this shot out of long, lush rough. Either use a more lofted utility wood or take a wedge and play out to the fairway.

9
SAND SAVVY

Gary Player prides himself on sand-play prowess.

Gary Player: a gutsy golfer with an incredible sand-play game.

Gary Player: the man in black. He used to dress that way because it gave him a sense of power. Today, at 5'7" and all of 147 pounds, he is one of the most powerful men in golf. When it comes to desire and the determination to overcome odds, Player is truly in a world of his own.

Player was born on November 1, 1936, in Johannesburg, South Africa, into the home of Harry Player, a miner. Gary Player's mother, Muriel, died when he was eight. As a youngster, Player was an avid sportsman, participating in rugby, cricket, track, swimming and diving. He played golf as well but never really became that enthusiastic about it until visiting the Virginia Park course. The club professional there was the father of Vivienne Verway, Player's future wife. By the time Player was 16, he became so serious about golf and making it his future profession that he used to stand in front of a mirror telling himself, "*I will be the best golfer in the world.*" At that point in his life, he began his mission, practicing literally from sunup to sundown.

In 1953, he turned pro and played the South African Tour. Not much happened at first; in fact, some so-called experts thought Player should give up the game, saying his swing was too flat and his grip too strong. Player proved them wrong, winning the 1955 Egyptian Matchplay, then the British Dunlop and South African Open in 1956. He finished fourth in the British Open that year, and that got him some attention. The educated galleries at the Hoylake links in England could see that Player was blessed with talent, particularly on and around the greens. Surprisingly, too, although he was slight, he hit the ball powerfully. Player let the press know that his strong hitting was due to a regular routine of exercise and a healthy diet.

In 1957, Player was invited to the Masters Tournament, played over the famous Augusta National course in Augusta, Georgia. He received the invitation in response to a letter his father had written to Clifford Roberts, the tournament chairman at the time. Player didn't play great golf, but he was enthused by that trip, particularly since he got to meet players such as Ben Hogan and Arnold Palmer. That same year, Player won the Australian PGA, beating Peter Thomson, one of the world's best players. In 1958, Player continued his fine play, winning the Australian Open and his first event in the United States, the Kentucky Derby Open. By this time, he was an established international player, traveling from country to country with his trusty bag of clubs.

1959 was a watershed year for Player—the highlight being his British Open win at Muirfield. Going into the last 36 holes of the final day, Player was eight strokes behind the leader. That didn't stop him. He fought back to win, proving that he had the heart of a lion. He had won his first major championship. Instead of resting on his laurels, Player practiced harder than ever, working to incorporate a couple of new movements into his swing to make it more efficient.

By 1961, Player was hitting the ball longer and straighter. Of course, he still had that brilliant short game to fall back on. That year, he won his second major championship: the Masters. He was the first overseas-based player to become the leading money winner on the American Tour circuit. In 1962, Player won the PGA, his third major championship. In 1965, Player won the U.S. Open at the Bellerive Country Club in St. Louis, Missouri, becoming one of only four players (Gene Sarazen, Ben Hogan and Jack Nicklaus are the others) to win all four major championships during their golf careers. Again, Player did not rest. Instead, he set a more than ambitious goal, a near impossible, if not highly improbable one of winning all four majors all over again.

He drew a step closer to attaining this goal in 1968 when he won the British Open at Carnoustie, in Scotland, after a final round battle with Nicklaus. Player won a total of seven times that year in Britain, South Africa and America and showed his dominance in the golf world by capturing the Picadilly World Matchplay Championship. In the three years that followed, he made more of a mark in America. He won the 1969 Tournament of Champions, the 1970 Greater Greensboro Open and the 1971 Jacksonville Open.

In 1972, he won the New Orleans Open. That year also brought his second PGA Championship win. Player had two majors under his belt, drawing a step closer to his goal of winning all four twice. He won the 1973 Southern Open and the 1974 Danny Thomas-Memphis. The highlights of 1974 were his second win at the Masters and third win at the British Open. Player was getting closer to accomplishing his four majors dream. To cap off the year, Player recorded the lowest score in a national championship at the Brazilian Open. His card read 3, 4, 3, 3, 4, 2, 3, 3, 4 (29); 2, 4, 3, 4, 4, 4, 2, 4, 3 (30). He shot 59!

He won the 1977 World Cup Individual, beating the very best players in the game. In 1978, he won the Tournament of Champions, the Houston Open and his third Masters (which actually put him only one PGA Championship and two U.S. Opens away from an unbelievable three-peat of the four majors). The style in which he won this championship reveals much about the character of Gary Player, as his playing partner, Seve Ballesteros, said:

In watching Gary burn up Augusta, I witnessed what many sportswriters still consider to be one of the all-time greatest comebacks in golfing history. Starting the day seven strokes behind tournament leader Hubert Green, Gary steadily closed the gap and actually willed victory. As he strode down the 13th fairway, he pointed to the giant gallery surrounding the green up ahead and said, "Seve, those people don't think that I can win, but you watch, I'll show them." And to my amazement, the short, but physically fit and mentally mature South African kept his promise. In probably the most sensational finish in Masters history (not forgetting Nicklaus' scorching last-round surge in 1976), Gary scored seven birdies over the last ten holes, shot 64 and took home the prestigious green jacket—a feat so phenomenal it left an indelible impression on my mind.

Player never accomplished his goal to win all the major championships twice; a second U.S. Open win eluded him. However, he won a total of nine major championships. He also won the South African Open 13 times, the Australian Open 7 times and the World Matchplay 5 times.

In 1985, at the age of 50, Player joined the Senior PGA Tour. Right off the bat, he won the Quadel Seniors Classic. It didn't take him long to win a major on that Tour either. In 1986, he won the PGA Seniors' Championship. A year later he won another major title, the United States Senior Open. Player has won a total of 18 Senior Tour titles and collected $3,954,084 in prize money. Knowing the competitive fire in this man, he's not done yet.

Aside from Player's strong will to win, his chief asset on the course has been his sand-play prowess. Player can afford to attack the flag, because even if he lands in the bunker there's an excellent chance that he'll save par, or maybe even hole out for birdie. You see, when he was young he would keep practicing sand shots until he had holed out five times. Sand shots cause most amateur golfers great anxiety and wasted strokes. If the bunker game is your nemesis, Gary Player's easy-to-learn, easy-to-repeat sand-play technique can help you shoot lower scores. Here's how it works.

Gary's Great Sand-Play Technique

In setting up to play sand shots, Player sets his right foot closer to the target line. This open address position allows him to more freely clear his left hip to the left on the downswing and swing the club through with his hands and arms. He puts about 60 percent of his weight on the left foot, and leaves it there throughout the swing to help him hit with a descending blow. Keeping his hands ahead of the ball, which is played pretty much opposite his left heel, also promotes a downward hit. He sets his head behind the ball to promote a high, soft-landing shot.

Going back, he picks up the club quickly with his hands and arms and allows his wrists to hinge freely. The swing is compact and upright. On normal bunker shots, you don't ever want to swing the club back on a flat plane.

Player's open stance and open clubface position help him lift the ball out of the sand.

SuperGolf

Player's compact upright swing is vital to his sand-play prowess.

Notice Player's solid takeaway action.

Player triggers the downswing by driving his legs laterally.

As Player's arms and hands drop down, he clears his left hip.

As the club approaches impact, Player concentrates on a contact spot in the sand, approximately two inches behind the ball.

Player hits down, letting the sand lift the ball out of the bunker.

Do that and you will swing down on a shallow arc, take too little sand and hit the ball over the green.

On the downswing, Player drives his legs laterally, then clears his left hip. He pulls the club down with his hands and arms and allows his wrists to unhinge in the impact zone. He drives the sand wedge into an area of sand about two inches behind the ball. The club slides through the sand under the ball, lifting it into the air. You never hit the ball. The ball takes a ride on the sand you cut out of the bunker.

FUTURE FAMER: CURTIS STRANGE

Ask any PGA Tour player who is the grittiest player out on the circuit today and they'll tell you Curtis Strange. Like Gary Player, Strange never gives up, and rest assured, he has the game to back up his competitive spirit and will to win.

Curtis Northrop Strange was born on January 10, 1955, in Norfolk, Virginia. His father owned the White Sands Country Club in Virginia Beach. It wasn't surprising that Strange took the game up seriously at the age of seven and later zoomed into a successful amateur career.

At age 18, he won the 1973 Southeastern Amateur. In 1974, he won the NCAA Championship and the Western Amateur. In 1975, he played on the American Walker Cup team, plus won the Eastern Amateur, the North and South Amateur and the Virginia State Amateur. The highlights of 1976 on the amateur circuit included repeats in the North and South and the Virginia State tournaments.

Strange turned pro in the spring of 1977. He admitted that competition was very different on the PGA Tour—even tougher than he expected. It only took winning his first tournament, the 1979 Pensacola Open, before he felt very comfortable competing among the world's best players. In 1980, he won the Houston Open and the Westchester Classic. He followed those with wins at the 1984 LaJet Classic and three 1985 tournaments: the Honda, the Las Vegas Invitational and the Canadian Open.

A bunker shot similar to this one helped Curtis Strange win the 1988 U.S. Open.

The Houston Open was his only win in 1986, but he exploded in 1987, winning the Canadian Open, the St. Jude Classic and the World Series of Golf. Strange was on top of his game, but he just couldn't take himself to that next level (even with the help of his coach, Jimmy Ballard) and win a major championship.

In 1988, he won the Independent Insurance Agent Open, the Memorial Tournament and the Nabisco Championship. While that was a very good year in itself, Strange made it a great year by winning the U.S. Open at the Country Club in Brookline, Massachusetts. The bunker shot that Strange hit on the 72nd hole to set up a par-putt conversion and earn a playoff bid against Nick Faldo proved to the world how talented a sand player he is. With a very high lip in front of him, Strange gripped the club very lightly, laid the clubface wide open, swung back to the halfway point with his hands and arms and then slapped the sand with the bounce of the club—as you should do. Out came the ball, flying fairly close to the hole. Strange had tied Faldo. He would beat him the next day for the title.

Strange did the impossible in 1989. He won the U.S. Open—*again*—at Oak Hill in Rochester, New York. Again, well executed bunker shots played a major role in his victory. Strange became the first pro golfer to win back-to-back U.S. Opens since Ben Hogan in 1950–1951. The young Virginian was now in a class all his own. And it got to him—the endorsements, the autographs, the phone calls, the pro-ams, the company days. Strange was burned out. He lost his enthusiasm for the game and his swing that served him so well. From 1990 to 1995, he finished no better than 41st on the money list. He also lost a critical match against Faldo in the 1995 Ryder Cup Matches, which probably cost America the Cup.

Strange is back now, playing with a good mental attitude and swing. Guaranteed, destiny will see him back in the winner's circle, and also in the Hall of Fame.

10
ROUGH AND READY

Tom Watson can hit the ball close to the hole—or into the cup—from any bad lie around the green.

Tom Watson: a man with a Huckleberry Finn look, and a killer instinct.

Entering the 1977 PGA Tour season, Jack Nicklaus had just come off one of his better years. He had won the World Series of Golf and the Tournament Players Championship, and was not about to give up his crown as the best player on the PGA Tour. Tom Watson had different plans. By the time the year was over, Watson had won three tournaments, plus two major championships—the Masters and British Open—beating Nicklaus and other true golfing greats. He topped the money list, earning $310,653. Watson was setting the high playing standards that all pro golfers would try to measure up to in years to come. Without question, a change of the guard had taken place. Watson had bumped Nicklaus off pro golf's pedestal.

Tom Watson was born September 4, 1949, in Kansas City, Missouri, a town that Watson loves so much he has never moved away. Ray Watson, who was a good player in his own right, taught his son the game at the early age of six. Ray stressed the importance of a good short game. He gave his son a cut-down putter and showed young Tom the correct way to grip the club. His father believed that if Tom learned the short stroke first, it would help him learn the long swing more quickly later on. Watson spent many hours on the putting green of the Kansas City Country Club trying to read breaks correctly and sink long putts or "snakes." The next club that Watson received from his father was a five iron that had also been cut down to suit him. Watson loved this club because he could now chip around the green. Watson played fantasy games in his head, making believe he had to get the ball up and down in two shots to win a U.S. Open. Little did he know that one day this dream would turn into reality.

Watson's game continued to improve through his high school years. He won the Missouri State Amateur four times, a record that still stands. Watson won the Kansas City Country Club championship and got to play against the hero of the day, Arnold Palmer, in an 18-hole match in 1964, the year that Palmer won the Masters. Watson played well in the match, having Palmer down after nine holes, but he faltered on the back nine to lose.

Tom Watson was clearly the best golfer to come out of Missouri. He decided to attend Stanford University and study psychology. Surprisingly, he never won the NCAA. In fact, he struggled to be the top player on his college team. During his senior year, Watson often drove over to the Monterey Peninsula to play Pebble Beach, then and now one of his favorite courses. Watson loved the holes near the ocean most. He would usually tee off early in the morning, when the dense fog crept inland, giving the course the appearance of St. Andrews in Scotland, the home of golf.

Watson joined the Tour in 1972, finishing a dismal 79th place on the money list. At that point, no one could have predicted what was in store for the Tour's version of Huck Finn. He played better in 1973, coming close to victory three times: The first three rounds of a tournament usually didn't give him much problem; the final round did. Consequently the media labeled Watson a "choker," a pro who couldn't play well in the heat of the battle. In 1974, after working with his idol, Byron Nelson, on his driving, Watson quieted the critics by winning the Western Open. The 1974 U.S. Open was Watson's to win, too, but his putting stroke suddenly let him down on day four. Watson finished fifth, and the media were at it again, saying he would never win a major championship because he couldn't play well on Sunday.

The 1975 U.S. Open was played at Medinah Country Club, and Watson lead after two rounds, shooting 135. He closed poorly however, shooting 78 and 77 in the final two rounds to finish ninth. Again the press had a field day. Watson finally silenced his critics three weeks later when he won the British Open at

Carnoustie in Scotland—the turning point of Watson's career. He dominated golf for the next decade.

In 1977, Watson won his first of two Masters, outdueling Nicklaus down the stretch in the final round. On the 71st hole of the championship, Watson sunk a doozie of a breaking putt from twenty feet for birdie. That score gave him the cushion he needed to coast to victory. Watson's win at Augusta was terrific. As it turned out, however, it wouldn't compare to his victory in the 1977 British Open, played at Scotland's Turnberry golf links. Both Watson and Nicklaus shot rounds of 68 and 70 to tie for the lead at the halfway point. On the final two days, these two legends were paired together and put on a show that the Scots—and golfers the world over—still talk about. In the third round, both golfers played brilliantly, each shooting a six-under score of 65. The stage was set for the young lion to beat golf's "Golden Bear." On Sunday, both Watson and Nicklaus played exceptionally well, neither one wanting to lose. It was truly a battle royal. But Watson emerged the victor, shooting a 65 to Nicklaus' 66 and beating the British Open scoring record by eight strokes.

Between 1977 and 1982, Watson won twenty-four times, but his greatest moment in the sun came when he won the 1982 U.S. Open—the title Watson wanted most to win. At age 33, time had been running out, until he discovered the Open would be played at his favorite American course, Pebble Beach. He hoped it would be his year to take home the bacon.

Cutting to the dramatics, Watson was tied with his old rival Nicklaus coming to the 71st hole, the 209-yard par-three 17th at Pebble. The Golden Bear had already finished his round and was sitting in the locker room watching Watson's every waggle on television. As usual, the wind was blowing, so Watson decided to play a two iron to the long green nestled between traps and the

Pacific Ocean. He also decided to attack the hole, to cut on the ocean side of the green. The fate of the Open rested on this shot, and Watson knew it. The swing he made was a little quick. He pulled the ball left of the green, 20 feet from the hole, in the heavy four-inch-high fringe grass. Once Watson surveyed the lie, he thought if he could only get the leading edge of the club under the ball, he could pop it up softly into the air and maybe land it close enough to the hole to save par. Watson knew that if he tried to finesse the shot, he would probably leave it in the wiry grass. If he got too aggressive he'd knock it over the green, score bogey or worse and lose the championship.

Before settling into a comfortably correct setup position, Watson took three practice strokes with a sand wedge, trying to determine, by memory, the proper swing tempo to use. Yes, memory. He had hit this very same shot before, on this very same hole, when he used to play Pebble Beach during his college days. Standing over the ball, he took a couple of deep breaths to relax his tense nerves. Then he swung. The ball popped gently into the air, landed on the green, then rolled into the cup. A birdie two, when, at best, he hoped to salvage par. What a bonus! Watson now had a one-stroke lead in the Open. But he still had hole 18 to play—a dogleg left par five that can give even the best players in the world trouble.

Watson split the middle of the fairway with his drive and decided to lay up short of the green with a seven iron. For his third shot, he played a nine iron and hit the ball twenty feet from the hole. On his putt, all he tried to do was lag it close for a sure par, and victory. But the ball found the cup. Tom Watson had won the Open by two strokes.

Before finishing his long hot streak of superb golf, Watson had won 32 PGA Tour titles and nine major championships. He was the PGA player of the year six times. Furthermore, he did what only Lee Trevino had been able to do before: match the great Jack Nicklaus stroke for stroke, on some of the world's finest courses in the world, and come out on top. In his prime, Watson drove the ball long and straight, hit high on-target irons and sunk long and short pressure putts. What stands out more than any other golfing asset, however, is Watson's ability to hit great shots from rough around the green, just as he had done at Pebble Beach in 1982. Watson spent years studying and practicing his craft, so let's see exactly what makes this Hall of Famer's wedge technique tick.

Tom Watson's Wedge Game Technique From Greenside Trouble

When facing a shot similar to the one at Pebble Beach's 17th hole, Watson selects a sand wedge because that club features around 55 degrees of loft and is heavier than a pitching wedge. These features of the sand wedge will allow you to loft the ball extra-softly into the air, provided you use a technique similar to Watson's.

At address, Watson sets the clubface open, although he raises it up off the grass, so as not to dislodge the ball and incur a two-stroke penalty. He also assumes an open stance and plays the ball forward in it. On the backswing, he swings the club outside the target line. The open stance helps him do this. The backswing action is quite wristy, because Watson wants to swing on an upright, rather than flat, plane. On the downswing, Watson swings the club across the target line to impart a degree of left-to-right cutspin on the ball—a type of spin that makes the ball stop very quickly, unless the greens are very firm from extreme exposure to sun and wind. To ensure that the club slides under the ball, with its face held wide open, Watson grips more firmly with the last three fingers of his left hand, and releases his right hand under his left hand, rather than over it, through impact.

One more final key: As Watson follows through, he tries to point the clubface toward the sky. Thinking of this image before you swing will further help you keep the clubface wide open in the hitting area and hit a wonderful soft-landing shot.

Watson's chip-in at Pebble Beach—one of the all-time great greenside shots.

Photo by Tony Roberts

FUTURE FAMER: LEE JANZEN

The one young player on the Tour today who knows no fear, and who finds a way to perform well under extreme pressure, is Lee Janzen. When the stakes are high and the going gets tough, Janzen rises to the occasion. On the course, he's truly as cool, calm and collected as an old Wild West gunslinger.

Janzen, born August 28, 1964, started playing golf seriously at the tender age of 14, after moving to Florida from Maryland. In Florida, he could play golf twelve months a year, and that suited him just fine. Janzen's first job was picking up range balls at the Imperial Lakes Country Club. Part of his pay was that he could hit as many balls as he liked. So, ironically, many of the balls he retrieved were ones he hit. Janzen learned to perform well under pressure by playing with older low-handicap players who knew the game. He bet them. The stakes were clear: If he didn't perform, the old-time veterans would "clean his clock."

Janzen attended Florida Southern College on a golf scholarship. He won the NCAA Division II Championship in typical Lee Janzen fashion, scoring birdie on five of the last nine holes.

While he turned professional in 1986, his first victory didn't come until the 1992 Northern Telecom Open. He followed that with a 1993 Phoenix Open win. But that victory would pale in comparison to what was on the horizon. Later that season, Janzen did something that no golfer had been able to do since Lee Trevino in 1968: shoot four rounds in the 60s in the U.S. Open, at the Baltusrol course in Springfield, New Jersey.

On the final day, with Tom Watson, Nick Price and Payne Stewart still contending for the trophy, Janzen found himself in trouble on the 16th hole, a 204-yard par three. After pulling his

SuperGolf

To hit a great recovery shot (like the one Lee
Janzen hit out of greenside grass during the
1993 U.S. Open), swing the club back on an
upright plane (above), then uncock your right
wrist and swing through the ball (right).

tee shot, Janzen faced a difficult chip. The ball was sitting down slightly in the second cut of fringe grass. To make matters worse, the green was lightning fast. Janzen knew that to hit the shot solidly he would have to keep his body still during the swing. So he put 70 percent of his weight on his left side, with the intention of keeping it there during the swing. Going back, he allowed his right wrist to cock early in the takeaway, allowing him to swing the club on the desired upright plane. On the way down, he simply uncocked the right wrist, causing the clubface to be delivered into the back of the ball.

Janzen hit the shot of a lifetime. The ball landed softly on the green, then trickled into the cup for a birdie. He finished with a total of 272, tying Jack Nicklaus' record for the lowest score ever shot in the Open. His Open win was certainly no fluke. He has since won the Tournament Players Championship, which many pros consider the "fifth" major. And, as his coach Rick Smith will tell you, Janzen's just getting warmed up.

11
CHIPPING MAGIC

If you had to bet on one man to hole a chip from manicured fringe grass, put your money on Ray Floyd.

Ray Floyd: from manicured fringe grass, he's dangerous.

When Ray Floyd starts something, he loves to finish it. Like a thoroughbred heading for the finish line, there is no holding him back. Floyd won for the first time on the PGA Tour in 1963, at age 20. He also won the 1992 Doral Open, at age 49. That tells you he can still beat the young "flat bellies," as well as his fellow Senior PGA Tour players. Floyd is a gifted athlete who has worked very hard to keep his game in shape. They talk about the eye of the tiger. Well, Floyd's truly got that. When he's in the hunt and he's got that familiar intense stare going, look out. He's coming to get you.

Ray Floyd was born September 4, 1942, in Fort Bragg, North Carolina, to a career Army man who loved golf almost as much as he loved his son. At age seven, Floyd started hitting balls at a driving range that his father had purchased at retirement. The range was the perfect place for Floyd to work on his swing. His father also taught him that the key to scoring on the golf course is knowing how to hit the wedge and chip shots. He told Ray not to chip with one club, but rather to let the lie of the ball dictate the club used for the shot. So Floyd experimented with the different lofted clubs in his bag, keeping track of how the ball reacted in the air and on the ground. He soon became an expert at hitting little chip shots. Floyd won more than his share of junior tournaments around the North Carolina area, but he reached a higher level when he captured the National Jaycee Junior Championship. In high school, Floyd played quarterback on the football team and was a star pitcher for the baseball team. In fact, in his senior year, Floyd was offered a major league contract from the Cleveland Indians, but he turned it down to concentrate on golf.

Floyd was offered the first golf scholarship at the University of North Carolina but dropped out of school after three months. He decided to follow in his father's footsteps and joined the

Army. After 18 months of Army life, he decided to try the PGA Tour. With the backing of nine business associates and his father, Floyd set out on a career that would lead him into the Hall of Fame. He missed the cut in the first ten tournaments he competed in, which is why he shocked himself and his backers when he won his eleventh tournament, the 1963 St. Petersburg Open. Floyd was the youngest man to ever win on the Tour since the 1920s and 1930s.

He won the 1965 St. Paul Open. In 1969, he won three times—the highlight being his PGA Championship victory at the NCR Country Club in Dayton, Ohio. But when Floyd started enjoying the nightlife, his career suffered a lapse. Shortly after his December 1973 marriage, however, his game started getting back on track. He won the 1975 Kemper Open.

In 1976, Floyd won the Masters, shooting a record score of 271. His trusty five wood helped him birdie the par-five holes. His superb chipping game salvaged crucial pars, particularly on the final day when greens were being missed literally left and right. Floyd also won the 1976 World Open. The next high point in Floyd's career was his 1982 PGA Championship win at Southern Hills, over good friend Lanny Wadkins.

In 1986, at the ripe age of 43, Floyd's dream of winning a U.S. Open Championship finally came true. Coming down the stretch at Long Island's Shinnecock Hills, Floyd played like a fearless youngster, battling eight top contenders for the title. In 1989, Floyd was selected by the PGA to captain the Ryder Cup Matches, being played that year at The Belfry in England. He loved being a leader so much that he took a break from Tour golf to prepare. The players responded to Floyd and conversed with him about strategy. The matches ended in a 14–14 tie. Several players wanted Floyd to captain the next team, but Floyd had his sights on the Senior Tour.

Floyd joined the PGA Senior Tour in 1992 and didn't waste any time becoming one of the best players on that Tour. He has already won over a dozen Senior events and three Senior Skins titles. Ray Floyd is a man to fear on the course, namely because of his fantastic chipping game. When the ball sits in the manicured fringe grass, he looks at the shot from all angles. But he's not thinking about hitting the ball close; hitting the ball close to the cup doesn't satisfy him. He tries to hole each chip with the determination of a boxer looking to score a knockout.

The reason Floyd is so proficient on chip shots has to do with a decision he made early on in his career. For every hour he spent practicing the full swing, he'd spend two hours working on the short game. Unlike the many pros who use a sand wedge for all chip shots, Floyd doesn't believe in using one club for all shots. Generally speaking, the longer the chip shot, the less lofted club he uses. Let's look at how a master plays this shot.

Floyd's Flawless Chipping Technique

Floyd's chipping setup resembles his putting stance and alignment. The feet are positioned close together, and aiming left of the target line. This "open" setup helps you swing the club nicely through the ball with your hands and arms. Floyd likes to stand tall with very little flex in his knees, because this also promotes a freer swinging action. He puts about 60 to 70 percent of his weight on the left foot and leaves it there throughout the stroke to promote a slight descending blow at impact. Playing the ball back in the stance with the hands ahead of the clubhead also promotes a downward hit, which propels the ball over the fringe grass, then starts it rolling as purely as a putt once it hits the green.

One chief reason that Ray Floyd is still a fantastic chipper is that he doesn't use a lot of wrist in hitting the ball. His swing motion is controlled almost entirely with the arms and shoulders. There might be some wrist-hinging action on the longer chip shots, but from nearby the hole, there's no wrist action at all in his swing. Floyd uses the image of a pendulum swinging to help him employ an even-tempo swing.

Floyd sets up to a chip similar to the way he sets up to a putt.

Floyd keeps his head still while swinging the club
back, a couple of feet past his right foot.

In the takeaway, Floyd's club lightly brushes the
grass.

SuperGolf

Floyd's start-down position.

Floyd's impact position.

Floyd's through-impact position.

Floyd's follow-through is virtually the same length as his backswing.

Going back, the club lightly brushes the grass, and stops when it passes his right foot by a couple of feet. Again, the arms and shoulders control the swinging action, while the head and body stay still.

On the downswing, all Floyd does is nudge a little more of his weight over to the left side. This helps him swing the club through smoothly, and nip the ball clearly off the short fringe grass. When looking at photographs of Floyd hitting a chip shot, you can see that the follow-through is virtually the same length as the backswing. A drill that Floyd worked on as a youngster was brushing the grass when taking practice swings. This encourages you to swing on a shallow arc so that you sweep the ball off the grass—not dig it out.

In the Doral Open a few years ago, Floyd was in a playoff with the great Jack Nicklaus. Floyd had just hit his ball over the green on the par-four 16th hole. Nicklaus looked like he had a birdie wrapped up: He was only twelve feet from the hole, and Nicklaus doesn't miss many from that distance. Floyd hadn't given up yet. Once Floyd saw the kind of lie he had, he thought for a minute, then visualized hitting the perfect chip shot. He didn't just see the ball finishing close to the hole. He saw it go in.

Floyd took out his club, played the ball back in the stance and used the same basic stroke he would use if his ball were on the green. The ball popped up over the fringe, landed on the edge of the green, then rolled right into the cup, for a birdie. Nicklaus was so surprised that he missed his putt, and Floyd was the champion.

Success is not measured by what happens at one moment. Success is measured by what you have accomplished over your career. Not many have accomplished what Ray Floyd has.

FUTURE FAMER: JOSE MARIA OLAZABAL

Jose Maria Olazabal was born February 5, 1966, in Fuenterrabia, Spain, to a mother and father who loved golf. Jose's father was the greenskeeper at the Royal San Sebastian Golf Course. Legend has it that Jose's mother was helping her husband change pin placements the night before her son was born. Olazabal started

Few modern-day players chip as well as Jose Maria Olazabal off manicured fringe grass.

playing golf as soon as he could walk, with a cut-down iron his father gave him. That explains why, at age seven, he beat older children to win the Spanish Junior Championship. At age 19, Olazabal won the European Tour Qualifying School. Not long after, he started playing golf for a living.

In his first year on Tour, 1986, Olazabal won the Ebel European Masters and the Sanyo Open to finish second on the Order of Merit. His star really started to shine in 1987, when he was picked by Tony Jacklin for the Ryder Cup team. Olazabal and fellow countryman Seve Ballesteros proved to a strong partnership, playing the Americans that year at Ohio's Muirfield Village. In the 15 Ryder Cup matches in which the two Spaniards have joined forces, their record is an impressive 13 wins and two losses. Olazabal's play has also been brilliant without the help of Seve. He won four points out of a possible five in the 1991 matches.

Olazabal hasn't just won on the European Tour. He has won four times on U.S. soil. When Olazabal won the 1990 World Series of Golf, he shot a score that, to this day, makes you wonder if he played all 18 holes. He shot a 61 at the Firestone Country Club, a course that measures 7,149 yards (from the tips).

In 1994, Olazabal became the second Spaniard to win the Masters. Olazabal is a gifted player, but the one area of the game where he is head and shoulders above everyone else is chipping. When laying a chip, from right off the edge of the green, Olazabal feels comfortable using the grip that he plays all his full shots with—the Vardon grip. Olazabal also grips down on the club for better feel and control. He sets his body open, or to the left of the target, to give himself a clear view of the hole and to encourage a free swinging action. The ball is played in the middle of his stance, with his weight on the left side. Before he swings, Olazabal pushes his hands slightly forward to help trigger a tension-free backswing action. In the backswing, the club moves away from the ball with the hands staying close to the body. If the hands move well away from the body, the tendency is to swing across the target line coming through, and pull the shot.

Olazabal's downswing action is aided by the movement of his right knee. The arms and shoulders start the club down. Then he rotates the right knee toward the target to help him accelerate the clubhead through the ball. In the hitting area, the clubhead stays low to the ground. He sweeps the ball off the turf, indicating a shallow arms-swing rather than an overly upright handsy swing. There's no flipping of the wrists as the club is coming down into the impact zone. Olazabal has beautiful tempo. He never tries to rush or force the club into the ball. A valuable tip that Olazabal got from Seve is to try to shave the ball off the grass using a level swing. Olazabal used to try to take a light divot, but now, thanks to Seve, he hits the ball more cleanly.

Jose Maria Olazabal is a Future Famer because he has proven he can take on the best players in the world and come out on top. He has a Ryder Cup record that is truly one of the greatest of all time. With one green coat hanging in his closet, he has the confidence to keep on winning major championships as long as he stays healthy.

12

PUTT FOR DOUGH

Billy Casper can still putt the eyes out of the hole.

In the 1960s, Billy Casper played in the shadow of three golf legends: Arnold Palmer, Jack Nicklaus and Gary Player. Casper was super-talented, yet he didn't quite catch the public's eye. He was the quiet type. Besides, he was battling Palmer for the top spot, and the public didn't like anyone who was trying to dethrone Arnie. It didn't matter, however, whether the public loved Billy Casper or not; the record books show that he was one of the greatest players of all time. And when the experts rate putters, Casper finishes at the top.

Billy Casper was born in San Diego, California, on June 24, 1931. He was the first of a long line of pros to polish their skills under the guidance of the San Diego junior golf program. While he was a proven all-around player years before he was able to shave, it was his short game and putting that caused people to take notice. After junior lessons were over, Casper used to take on the instructors in a little game of seeing who could get the ball up and down from thirty yards the most times in a row. Casper won these contests almost every time. He possessed superb touch and feel for playing short shots. It was as though the club and his body blended together. He knew just how far to swing the club back, and how fast to swing it down to hit the ball close to the flag. The ironic thing was, on those rare occasions when he hit the ball much farther away from the hole than the others, he would sink the putt.

Casper worked hard on his game, believing that regular practice would eventually allow him to play golf for a living. Through the junior golf program, he played some of the best courses in Southern California, competing with and beating the best the area had to offer. When he turned thirteen, he entered the Emerald Hills Golf Club tournament, his first competition. Casper shot 80, which was a personal best by a good many shots. The problem was, he had entered the tournament with a handicap of 24. The tournament committee believed he hadn't been honest with his handicap, so they disqualified him.

After serving in the military for a few years, Casper turned professional in 1954. Initially, he struggled with his game, because he always hit drives off the tee, and he swung too fast. Before long, though, Casper learned to tee off with a three wood or long iron on narrow holes, just to keep the ball in play. He slowed down his tempo, too. These changes paid off. That same year, Casper captured his first PGA victory, the Labatt Open.

During the next few years, Casper continued his winning play, greatly wanting to realize his childhood dream of winning a major championship. In 1959, his dream came true. He won the U.S. Open at the Winged Foot Golf Club in Mamaroneck, New York. Coming into the event, his drives were straight and his irons on target, but his putting was not up to par. He decided to try a new putter—usually a cardinal sin. The switch worked wonders: He one-putted 31 times over the 72 holes, a performance that earned him a one-stroke victory over Bob Rosburg. Casper loved his new putter and he went on to win four times in 1959.

In the 1966 U.S. Open, played at San Francisco's famed Olympic Club, Casper trailed the king of golf, Arnold Palmer, by seven shots with nine holes to play. It looked like Casper was playing for second place—until his putter caught fire. Playing like a man possessed, he couldn't miss on the greens. He shot 68 to tie Palmer, earning an 18-hole playoff the following day.

Needless to say, in that playoff Casper was the underdog, Palmer the crowd favorite. Casper proved he wasn't intimidated by the crowd or by Palmer, posting a solid 69 to win his second Open trophy by four shots. He never got the praise he deserved for that victory. Sadly, it was always the Open that Palmer lost, instead of the Open that Casper won. The truth is, Casper shot

68 in the final round and 69 in the playoff, on a super-test of golf against Palmer. So he deserved more respect.

In 1970, Casper won a third major: the prestigious Masters, played over the challenging Augusta National course in Georgia. That victory did not come without a playoff battle either. Casper's opponent was Gene Littler, another golfer who had come up from the ranks of the San Diego junior program. The greens at Augusta are notoriously fast and undulated. Still, they failed to stop Casper from holing birdie putts. He shot a 69 to beat his childhood friend by four strokes and captured his one and only green jacket.

During his time on the regular Tour, Casper went about his business in a serious—and some say, eccentric—way. He had his caddie stand a certain distance from the ball; the bag had to be tilted at a certain angle; the club waggled a certain number of times before each swing. One time, when he felt that he needed to lose weight to return to good playing form, he even went on a diet of buffalo burgers and bear steaks. This approach might have cost Casper a few fans, but the results were what put him into the Hall of Fame. Casper won 51 PGA tournaments. He competed on eight Ryder Cup teams. He won the Vardon Trophy, for the lowest scoring average on Tour, five times. He won Player of the Year twice. He won the PGA Tour money title in 1966 and 1968.

Billy's Superb Putting Stroke

Casper believes that the key to great putting is to let the left hand control the stroke to make sure that the left hand leads and the right hand follows. Casper recommends using a reverse overlapping grip. In assuming this putting hold, let the first finger of the left hand rest on top of the little finger of the right hand. There are a lot of variations of the reserve overlap grip, but this is the unique one with which Casper won two Opens.

At address, Casper believes that the closer the hands and arms are to the body, the better chance you will have of delivering the putterface squarely to the ball. When you reach for the ball, the arms tense up, causing you to mishit the putt. Casper allows his arms to bend more than other pros. The reason is, he feels this further helps him keep tension out of his hands and wrists. Part of Casper's left hand rests on the inside of his left thigh, and it barely moves during the stroke. This helps him keep the putterface dead square to the hole, on the backswing and the downswing.

Casper's eyes are directly over the target line, because this position promotes a straight-back, straight-through stroke. (If your eyes are well inside the target line, it's more difficult to keep the putterface square to the hole. The putter moves along an exaggerated in-to-out path, often causing the ball to be pushed right of the hole.) Casper's stance is slightly wider than the width of his shoulders, and he distributes his weight equally: 50 percent on the ball of his left foot, 50 percent on the ball of his right. He finds that this stance enhances his balance and gives him the solid foundation that's needed to make a pure stroke. Playing the ball opposite his left hand allows him to return the putterface to the back center portion of the ball.

Casper's backswing action is very simple, yet very effective. To trigger it, he pushes the putter back with his left hand while simultaneously hinging his right wrist. The pushing action of his left hand is so gentle, and the backswing so short, that the left hand remains "hugging" the inside portion of his left thigh. Casper perfected this pushing action by hitting putts with his left hand on the club, his right hand behind his back. He preferred to practice this drill when the greens still had dew on them from the night before. That way, he could monitor the initial path of the putterhead by looking at the mark it left on the wet grass behind the ball.

Casper controls the downswing with his right wrist. The faster he unhinges the right wrist, the faster the putterface returns to the ball and the farther the ball rolls. Casper had this pop stroke down pat, having devoted hours to its practice. This explains why he was such a good lag putter, especially on putts over 30 feet.

Casper's Putting Stroke: Caught on Camera

Casper in his putting address position.

SuperGolf

Casper starting his downswing.

Casper at the end of his backswing.

Casper at the completion of his stroke.

Casper swinging through the impact zone.

FUTURE FAMER: BEN CRENSHAW

Every so often, a player comes along who looks like he can't miss on the greens. Throughout golf history, that tag has belonged to Billy Casper and Jack Nicklaus, of course, but also Bobby Jones, Bobby Locke, Bob Charles, Arnold Palmer and, believe it or not, Tom Watson, who now suffers occasionally from the "yips." For the last decade, Ben Crenshaw has been the man with the magic wand. From the time Texas-born Crenshaw won the Texas State Boys Championship at age 15, golfers have expected great things from "Gentle Ben." One person who never had doubts that Crenshaw would make it big was the late Harvey Penick, his lifelong coach.

Crenshaw attended the University of Texas, and while there, he won the NCAA Individual Championship three times. In 1973, Crenshaw decided to turn professional. After finishing first in the PGA qualifying school (winning by 12 strokes), he entered the San Antonio-Texas Open, his first PGA Tour event. The most knowledgeable members of the golf press were not suprised when Crenshaw putted his way to victory.

During the 1970s, Crenshaw fit right in. He had long blond hair like Jack Nicklaus and Johnny Miller. But something happened on the way to greatness. He didn't win any of the four major championships. So, rather unjustly, some television golf commentators started calling him a "bridesmaid." In all fairness, Crenshaw had some personal and physical problems, but that didn't seem to matter to him. Crenshaw learned the hard way that, in America, nobody remembers who finishes second. Crenshaw remained feisty, however, never giving up mentally and practicing harder than ever. Still, it wasn't until 1984 that his time in the limelight came.

After three rounds of the year's Masters, Crenshaw was two strokes behind leader Tom Kite, his former college roommate.

Crenshaw swings the putter back (above), *then through* (right), *on a flat arc.*

There was no reason to think that Crenshaw would win. He had come close in majors before, finishing second five times. The Masters, golf experts always say, starts on the back nine, and the tenth hole is where contenders often start folding like cheap card tables. The tenth hole is a 485-yard par four, with a green that is so super-slick, it's one of the most difficult to putt on.

On the final day, Crenshaw had the lead when he stood on the tenth tee. He decided, after careful thought, to play an aggressive drive down the right side of the fairway and let the ball draw back to the center of the fairway. He hit the shot exactly as planned, leaving himself in the best possible spot to fix his second shot at the flagstick. That wasn't to be. He hit an indifferent approach that left him 60 feet from the cup. You could tell by the sounds coming from the gallery that they figured Crenshaw was starting to choke. After all, Crenshaw had left himself such a difficult putt that even he would probably three-putt and lose the lead. Not true.

As usual, Crenshaw stood tall at address, with his arms hanging down naturally. The putter swung well inside the target line on the backswing and was delivered squarely to the ball. The ball started its roll along the target line, kept rolling and rolling, then fell into the cup. Crenshaw went on to win that Masters. Since that time, he has won nine more tournaments, including a second Masters in 1995. Most of those wins can be credited to Crenshaw's unique putting stroke.

Most pros swing the putter back along the target line, then through on the same path. Crenshaw, on the other hand, swings the club on an inside-square-inside path. His argument is, it's the same path along which he swings every other club, so he's used to it.

If your straight-back, straight-through putting stroke isn't working, try swinging the club on a flatter arc, using a long, flowing arms-shoulders stroke like Crenshaw's.

13

LADY LEGENDS

What you can learn from distinguished women Hall of Famers Mickey Wright and Nancy Lopez.

Mickey Wright: One of the All-Time Great Drivers

Mickey Wright just may be the greatest woman golfer of all time, with the greatest swings ever. By the time her career was over, she had won 82 tournaments—44 of these in a four-year span. She won the prestigious U.S. Open four times. She also shot the lowest score in an LPGA event: a 62 in the 1962 Midland Texas Open.

Mickey was born to Kathryn and Arthur Wright. Her father, a successful attorney from San Diego, encouraged her to play ball sports at an early age. That helped her develop superb hand-eye coordination. Wright fell in love with golf at the age of 11 after

Mickey Wright: during her heyday, her smile was as sweet as her swing.

hitting balls at the driving range with her father. She would hit balls by the hour, swinging as hard as she could on each shot. John Bellante, the golf professional at the La Jolla Country Club, gave Wright her first lesson. He could see that she had talent, even though it was raw at that point.

In 1952, Wright won the United States Golf Association Junior Championship at the Monterey Peninsula Country Club. This victory proved that she could beat the best players the United States had to offer. She was on her way. When she turned professional in 1955, she won $6,325 in prize money and ended up 12th on the money list. But to Wright, playing professional golf was never about winning money; she loved to win titles.

Wright broke through in 1956, winning the Jacksonville Open. She won three times in 1957. She won the 1958 U.S. Open and the LPGA Championship in the same year—the first time that feat had ever been accomplished. In 1963, Wright won 13 times, a record that will probably never be matched or beaten. She created an excitement in women's golf that had never been seen before. She had a picture-perfect swing and a great short game. Every man and woman in the country wished they could hit a ball like Mickey Wright. She was one of the few players who made golf look easy. During her glory days, Wright worked harder than anyone on her game. She spent a lot of time with some of the top teachers, learning as much about the swing as possible. When traveling, golf was the first thing on her mind when she woke up and last thing on her mind when she retired to bed.

The secret to Wright's sensational record was her ability to drive a ball powerfully and accurately. She was like a machine. She had a swing that was repeatable and quite beautiful to watch.

Mickey's Magnificent Swing

Wright played out of a square stance and balanced her weight evenly on the balls of her feet. Her stance was slightly wider than her shoulders, as she felt this promoted good balance. She placed her hands slightly behind the ball to aid a one-piece takeaway, with the arms and shoulders, and a wide swing arc. She positioned the ball relatively forward in her stance to encourage an upswing hit.

Wright had one of the widest, most powerful swing arcs of any woman golfer who ever played the game. That's because she delayed the hinging action of her right wrist. It wouldn't start cocking until she had transferred most of her weight to the inside of her right heel. Wright also generated great power through her wonderful turning actions. At the top of the swing, her shoulders were coiled about 100 degrees, her hips about 50 degrees. Her coiling action was so strong, her left heel came well off the ground. The club was just short of the parallel position. Being a little more compact, she claimed, gave her more control of the club—and shot. To trigger the downswing, Wright replanted her left heel, then uncoiled her hips and shoulders. As she uncoiled her body, her arms delivered the club powerfully into the ball. To encourage a strong upswing hit, Wright kept her head behind the ball through impact.

A drill that Wright practiced throughout her career was hitting balls out of light rough with a wood. This helped her driving game because it forced her to stay down and hit the ball with a powerful sweeping action. She had an energy-efficient swing that was always in balance. She loved to compete, and was seldom pleased with second place. Her inner drive to be the best gave her a place in the Hall of Fame.

Mickey's Wood Drill: It Can Help You Groove the "Wright" Swing Technique

Step One: Set up with your hands slightly "behind" the ball.

Step Two: Swing the club back to the halfway point, keeping the wrists "quiet."

SuperGolf

Step Three: Swing back, coiling your shoulders to the max and letting your left heel come off the ground.

Step Four: Replant your left heel to trigger the downswing action.

Step Five: Uncoil your hips and deliver the club into the ball with a powerful sweeping action.

Future Famer: Laura Davies

Laura Davies was born in Coventry, England, on October 5, 1963. When she was a teenager, her brother introduced her to golf. She fell in love with the sport straight away and loved to practice. She would play a certain shot fifty or one hundred times until she got it just right. Davies turned professional in 1985 and won her first tournament, the Belgian Open. The year of 1987 turned out to be one of Davies' biggest. She won the U.S. Open and the Italian Open, playing brilliant golf from tee to green.

Golfing fans would rather follow Davies than just about anyone else. It's fun to watch her tee it up, knowing that she will hit the ball places that no other woman ever has. Although she hasn't reached her peak yet, she was still the LPGA's leading money winner in 1994 and the second leading money winner in 1995, and she's been hot in 1996. Watch Davies' swing and the words "tremendous power" and "solid balance" will come to mind. Let's look at her long-hitting secrets.

Laura Davies: a "powerful" force on the LPGA Tour

LAURA'S LONG-DRIVING TECHNIQUE

At address, Davies sets the ball on a tuft of grass rather than a tee. The reason: Grass will intervene between the ball and clubface at impact, causing the shot to fly twenty yards farther than normal. Davies points both her feet perpendicular to the target line, unlike her contemporaries who fan both feet outward about 20 to 25 degrees. This positioning allows Davies to make a powerful backswing turn without swaying, and hit powerfully against a firm left side.

Davies produces added power by hitting the ball off a tuft of grass rather than a tee peg.

Davies' powerful backswing arc is produced by a big upper body turn. She rotates her left shoulder fully under her chin and coils her hips to the max in a clockwise direction. Davies depends on a lateral slide of the lower body to trigger the downswing action. As weight shifts to her left side and the hips clear, she keeps her head behind the ball and resists with her lower body. This resistance (holding the upper body back, while the lower body drives) increases the speed of her arms and club, and is responsible for her huge power.

Davies hits the ball so long off the tee that she reaches par-five holes in two shots—with irons. With that kind of power, there's no doubt Davies will be exciting galleries for years to come, and one day enter Florida's "Great Hall."

Nancy Lopez: One of the All-Time Great Putters

Nancy Lopez was born January 6, 1957, in Torrance, California. At age seven, she received a cut-down three wood from her father, Domingo. Right away, she started hitting balls around the yard. At the age of nine, she won her first tournament—by 110 strokes! It wasn't unusual for Lopez to practice all day long. Her father was her biggest fan. He would work all day and then spend time with her on the range and putting green. He also helped her set goals.

Lopez won the New Mexico Women's State Amateur and the United States Girls title when she was just 12 years old. She attended the University of Tulsa on a full golf scholarship and tied for second place in the U.S. Open when she was an amateur. In 1977, she joined the LPGA Tour.

It didn't take Lopez long before she proved to the world that she was ready to be the number one player on Tour. She won

Nancy Lopez: known for her warm personality and hot putting stroke.

$161,235 in her first year—the most money any rookie had ever pocketed. She was named LPGA Player of the Year and LPGA Rookie of the Year. Plus, she won the Vare Trophy for the lowest scoring average. In her first two seasons on the Tour, she won 17 tournaments, including five in a row. To date, Lopez has won over 45 tournaments and is certain to be remembered as one of the greatest players—and putters—of all time. She is a perfect role model for any athlete, male or female. Some call her the Arnold Palmer of the LPGA circuit.

SuperGolf

Nancy's Near-Perfect Putting Stroke

Lopez uses the interlocking grip. For added control of the putter, she points her right index finger down the right side of the club-shaft. Her alignment is "square," meaning she sets her feet, knees,

In the takeaway, Lopez moves the putter virtually straight back along the ball-hole line.

Lopez points her right index finger down the right side of the clubshaft. This maximizes her control of the putterhead on the backswing and downswing.

hips and shoulders parallel to the ball-hole line. Lopez has tested this setup position and feels it promotes a square-to-square stroke. To reduce tension in her arms, Lopez bends them quite dramatically. She also keeps her elbows in close to her body, to enhance her control and consistency.

On the downswing, Lopez moves the putterhead along the target line (left) *and keeps the follow-through short* (below).

Lopez's backswing is controlled by her hands. The putter moves virtually straight back, and stays low to the ground. The right wrist hinges slightly as the putterhead swings back along the target line. Her thoughts are to keep the arms quiet and let the hands and wrists do the work. Lopez grew up playing golf on a municipal course in New Mexico that featured slow greens. She developed a somewhat wristy "pop stroke" to help her handle these conditions. Here's how that stroke works on the downswing:

The right wrist unhinges, allowing the putterface to be delivered down along the target line squarely into the ball. Because Lopez uses a hit-and-hold downswing technique, her follow-through is extra-short. This stroke has worked well for Lopez. She thinks amateurs should copy it because when you use the wrists in the downswing, you don't have to take the putter back quite as far as you do when using a total-arms stroke. Lopez's argument: The shorter the backswing, the better your chances of employing an easy-to-repeat straight-back, straight-through stroke.

When Lopez retires, the game will lose one of its favorite women players. The good news is, this Famer has hit so many good shots that we're guaranteed to be left with fond golfing memories.

FUTURE FAMER: JAN STEPHENSON

Jan Stephenson is a flamboyant gallery favorite who is as exciting to watch as any player on tour. Stephenson's game is a lot like Johnny Miller's was in the 1970s. When she is hot, she is a birdie machine. When she is struggling, her scores soar. This native Australian came to the United States long before Crocodile Dundee and Greg Norman, and she has had about as much suc-

Jan Stephenson: She has never lost the winning spirit.

cess as the other two. With sixteen Tour titles under her belt, and the respect of her fellow pros for being one of the best putters on the LPGA Tour, Stephenson is far from finished.

She was born December 22, 1951, in Sydney, Australia. She became the first woman to win the Wales Schoolgirl Championship five times and the New South Wales Junior Championship three times. She also won the Australian Junior Championship three times. Stephenson wasn't just one of the best players in Australia; she was *the* best player in Australia. She dominated golf as it had never been dominated before. That's why she was eventually voted by the press Woman Athlete of the Year in 1971.

Before Stephenson decided to come to the United States and prove to herself that she really had "it," she played on the Australian Tour. The ladies on the Aussie Tour were good, but they were no match for Stephenson. Their games weren't polished like Stephenson's. Her putting is what set her apart from the other Aussie players. She won four times on the Australian Tour and knew it was time to head to the States. Stephenson made a big splash when she joined the LPGA Tour in 1974. The Tour was ready for a new face. With her solid game and charm, the Tour had found a player that the crowds would come out in masses to follow. Stephenson was voted Rookie of the Year.

The following two years she finished in the top twenty-five, winning two events: the Sarah Coventry and Birmingham classics. Stephenson was on the cover of every golf magazine in the country, and quite a few that weren't golf related. She was the LPGA's hottest property. One of the goals that Stephenson had set for herself when she started out was to win a major championship on the LPGA Tour. That goal was realized when she shot 279 to win the 1979 LPGA Championship. In 1983, she won a second major—the U.S. Open. Although her game slipped during the 1990s, her teacher, Gary Smith, has been getting her swing back on track.

One part of Stephenson's game that is looking real good is her putting. Her stroke is your basic square-to-square arms-shoulders action, but the way she grooves it, and keeps it fine-tuned, is unique. When practicing putting, she works on these two drills, which you'd be smart to incorporate into your own practice sessions.

DRILL ONE Place a plastic ball marker upside down on the putting green, approximately a foot behind the ball. You want the side with the stem to point upward. Swing back, trying to brush

Stephenson's ball-marker drill trains you to keep the putter low to the ground in the backswing.

the stem. If you hit the marker, you know you're employing a nice wristless backswing. If you miss the marker, it means you overcocked the wrists and lifted the putter up on too steep an angle. You want the putter to stay low to the ground on the backswing.

DRILL TWO Hit putts with a sand wedge. If you employ a smooth, wristless downswing, and swing the club straight through along the target line, the leading edge of the wedge will hit the ball solidly. If, however, you chop at the ball or decelerate your

Stephenson's sand wedge drill trains you to swing through along the target line while keeping your wrists locked.

arms, you'll fail to make solid contact. The result: a push to the right of target.

When Jan Stephenson first played the LPGA Tour, she was known as a glamour gal. She quickly stopped that talk by entering the winner's circle quite often. When people mention her name now, they talk about what a great champion she is, instead of how beautiful she is.

14

SHOTMAKING WIZARDRY

Chi Chi Rodriguez is the ultimate shotmaking model.

Chi Chi Rodriguez: when it comes to working the ball, he's in a class of his own.

Chi Chi Rodriguez was born October 23, 1935, in Bayamon, Puerto Rico. He was born poor. He loved golf from the time he was a very young boy, but all he could do to satisfy his appetite was sit high in a tree and watch the millionaires drive into the country club and walk with their caddies around the course. Rodriguez played golf, too, but instead of using shiny new clubs, he had a guava stick with a crushed tin can for a ball. You can only imagine the joy on this young poor boy's face when, at around age 10, he was given a five iron and a real ball.

When Rodriguez looks back, he does so with no regrets. He thanks God that he was at least given the tools to make something of himself. Moreover, what may appear to be a backward way of learning the game turned out to be an advantage. Hitting the tin can with the guava stick, and practicing with the five iron, sharpened Rodriguez's hand-eye coordination and heightened his sense of touch. One-club golf taught him to work the club on various paths and planes, at varying speeds, because this is the only way you can improvise and hit an array of shots with a five iron.

Working the ball from right to left, left to right, low and high, was in Rodriguez's blood by the time he was a teenager playing a real course with a full set of clubs. Frankly, he hated hitting straight shots—so much so, that even if his ball was in the middle of the fairway and the pin was in the middle of the green, he'd draw or fade the shot toward the pin, just for fun. When he strayed from the fairway, and the ball was in the middle of a group of trees, he loved the challenge of hitting a well-executed imaginative shot onto the green. Rodriguez played so well that, at age 17, he finished only one stroke behind the winner in the Puerto Rico Open.

Rodriguez's skills got the attention of some wealthy business-men, who felt so strongly that he should turn pro that they backed him. They had a good horse. In 1963, three years after turning pro, Rodriguez won the Denver Open. The following year, he took two tournaments: the Lucky International and the Western Open. His next win was the 1967 Texas Open. From the years 1968 to 1979, he won only four more tournaments—Sahara Invitational (1968), Byron Nelson Classic (1972), Greater Greensboro Open (1973) and Tallahassee Open (1979). All the same, Rodriguez was nearly always in the money, thanks to his long drives (he sometimes hit the ball 300 yards off the tee) and his outstanding shotmaking skills. But he was a streaky putter. Only if his putting was hot would he take home the first-place purse.

When Rodriguez sunk a putt, he would throw his straw hat over the hole, as if to say he had the ball trapped. Then he would do a little dance around the green. In those days, Rodriguez was known as the "Clown Prince" of the Tour. Back then, golf wasn't as loose a sport. Consequently, some players nicknamed Rodriguez "Four-Stroke Penalty," because when they were paired with him their concentration was so bad it usually cost them four strokes. Rodriguez has since changed his routine. (Nowadays, when a putt drops, he pretends his putter is a sword, making the gestures of a matador finishing off a ball. His fellow pros and the gallery love it.)

Playing golf on the PGA Tour earned Rodriguez just over a million dollars. Not bad for a poor boy from Puerto Rico who was formerly a country club shoe-shine boy and caddie master. He was to do even better for himself.

In late 1985, Rodriguez joined the Senior PGA Tour, and almost right away, his game reached a new level. Even the putts started dropping. He was so hot, and so many people started talking about his exceptional shotmaking skills, that Jack Nicklaus sent his son Jackie to Rodriguez for lessons. Jackie, who was a young pro at the time, learned an impressive collection of shots. His father, the one and only Jack Nicklaus, became interested and wanted Jackie to show him those shots. Jackie did. To shorten a long story, Jack Nicklaus has gone on record as saying those supershots helped him win the 1986 Masters.

After a great 1986, Rodriguez finished first on the money list the following year. His earnings: $509,145. Rodriguez was rolling—and he continued to roll. His victories included the 1988 Digital Seniors Classic, the 1989 Crestar Classic, the 1990 Las Vegas Senior Classic, the 1991 GTE West Classic, the 1992 Ko Olina Senior Invitation and the 1993 Burnett Classic.

In just eleven years on the Senior PGA Tour (1985–1995), Rodriguez has won 22 tournaments, earning over 5 million dollars.

Chi Chi's Shotmaking Wizardry

At 5'7", 130 pounds, Rodriguez proves that you don't have to be big to play great golf. Here are three shots that have made him famous and instructions for playing them.

THE RISER This sand-wedge shot is ideal when the ball lies in the fairway around 40 yards from the hole. The ball will rise quickly into the air, then stop the split second it hits the green. It's particularly useful when playing to greens that are extra-firm and fast running due to excessive exposure to hot sun and wind. Here's how Rodriguez plays this shot.

ADDRESS Play the ball forward in an exaggerated open stance. Lean your upper body away from the target, and leave it like that throughout the swing, since this will help you hit the ball softly into the air.

SuperGolf

Rodriguez is such an uncanny shotmaker that he can make the ball rise quickly, then "dance" in the air.

BACKSWING Swing the club outside the target line. Stop when the club reaches the halfway point. The higher you want to hit the shot, the more you should allow your wrists to hinge.

DOWNSWING Swing the club across the ball. To ensure a floating shot that dances in the air and stops quickly on the green, allow the clubhead's heel to lead its toe in the hitting area.

TAILORING THE TIP Practice this shot until you learn to accelerate the clubface underneath the ball. Trust that the club's loft will pop it into the air. Trying to help the ball up or getting tentative through impact will cause you to skull the shot.

THE POWER-FADE DRIVE This is the ideal shot to play when the hole winds from left to right, or "doglegs" right. Essentially, it will allow you to cut off distance. In turn, by shortening the hole, you put yourself in position to hit a more lofted club into the green, and score birdie more easily.

ADDRESS In gripping, hold the handle of your driver more firmly than usual with your left hand. Ultimately, this encourages a delayed release of the hands and keeps the clubface from turning over through impact. Tee the ball lower than normal, too; the top of the ball should be even with the top of the clubface. Teeing the ball low promotes the upright swing plane you desire for hitting a power fade. Aim your feet, knees, hips and shoulders—and the clubface—to the left of your final target. The more you want the ball to curve, the more open your body and clubface alignment.

BACKSWING Basically, use your normal swinging action. The only thing you should do· differently is swing to the three-quarter point, instead of to the classic parallel position. This compact backswing will prevent you from overcocking your wrists at the top and releasing the club early on the way down.

DOWNSWING Shift your weight to your left side. As the clubhead approaches the ball, clear your left hip, but keep your head behind the ball. Maintain your firm left-hand grip pressure through impact—that's what allows you to hold the clubface slightly open at impact and impart fade-spin on the ball.

THE SOFT DRAW This is the perfect shot to hit when facing a medium iron into a par-four hole, and the pin is tucked in the left-hand corner of the green behind a big bunker.

ADDRESS Grip the club lightly in the fingers of both hands. This type of grip will enhance the releasing action of your hands, allowing the toe end of the club to lead its heel through impact, and imparting right-to-left draw-spin on the ball. Aim the club-face at the middle of the green, where you want the ball to start its flight. Aim your body toward your final target: the flag situated in the left-hand corner of the green.

BACKSWING Rotate your hips and shoulders in a clockwise direction. Swing the club back on an exaggerated flat path.

DOWNSWING Uncoil your left hip, then rotate your right forearm over your left more quickly than normal. Again, this exaggerated releasing action turns the clubface over, thereby imparting over-spin on the ball. The ball will start flying toward the middle front portion of the green, then turn softly to the left before landing and rolling toward the hole.

Rodriguez's shots have earned him a spot in the Hall of Fame, and he'll be exciting galleries for years to come. However, there's some new, young blood coming up.

Future Famer: Ernie Els

Theodore Ernest Els was born October 17, 1969, in Johannesburg, South Africa, the same city as golfing great, Gary Player. Player thinks Els is the next world beater. Few golf experts disagree with that prediction. He started playing golf at age nine. At age 13, he beat Phil Mickelson in the Junior World Championship in San Diego. Back then, Els was also an accomplished tennis player. Wanting to make a living from playing sports professionally, Els had to decide between golf and tennis. He chose golf. Judging from his huge success already, it's obvious he made the right decision. Standing 6'3" and weighing 215 pounds, Els uses his strength to his advantage, particularly off the tee. In fact, he's one of the few players who can pretty much keep up with John Daly. Like Daly, Els has a pair of soft hands. Maybe they were in his genes. Maybe he got those from hitting so many dying lob shots over the net of his backyard tennis court as a kid. One thing is certain, those hands have enabled him to hit wonderful shots.

Els' 1994 U.S. Open win has been his biggest to date. At the time of his victory, few on this side of the Atlantic had ever heard of him, even though he had already made his mark elsewhere. He had chalked up six home wins, including the triple crown of golf: the South African Masters, Open and PGA. He had won in Japan and also on the European Tour. Even more impressively, before his U.S. Open win at Oakmont, he finished in the top ten in five of the eight majors he had played in. Later in 1994, Els showed his stuff by winning the World Matchplay Championship, at the Wentworth Golf Club in England. In that tournament, he beat some great players, including Seve Ballesteros, Jose Maria Olazabal and Colin Montgomerie.

Els is not big on lessons or on practice. He thinks most American players are overcoached. However, David Leadbetter of the Lake Nona Golf Club in Orlando, Florida, does help from time to time with his setup and minor swing tune-ups. Ernie played virtually full time on the PGA Tour in 1995, having a fine season. He won the Byron Nelson Classic and finished 14th on the money list, earning $842,590. He'll continue to focus his attention on the American Tour—he's building a house at Lake Nona where Leadbetter, who also teaches Nick Faldo, lives. Maybe Els will feel compelled to visit the lesson tee more often.

Ernie Els depends on active hip action to produce powerful tee shots.

There's no question that Els has the talent to win many more major championships and establish himself as the world's number one player. Right now, it's just a question of how soon he'll rise to the top. The great thing about his shotmaking game is his ability to hit powerful drives and iron shots and hit wonderful short touch shots from close by the greens.

To generate power like Ernie Els, from the tee and from the fairway, simply turn your left shoulder behind the ball on the

Ernie Els' smooth swing—he lets the club do the work—allows him to hit on-line pitch shots.

backswing. On the downswing, turn your right hip and knee toward the target, as Els does in the illustration on page 210. Even if you are of small stature, these two keys will enable you to hit the ball farther than you ever have before.

In hitting pitch shots—anywhere from 60 yards in from the green—let the club do the work. Swing the club smoothly. To help you do that, tell yourself to *let the ball get in the way of a good swing.*

Three other important keys for playing the pitch shot like Els:

1. Setting up with 60 percent of your weight on your left foot.
2. Gripping firmly with the left hand.
3. Rotating the back of your left hand, and the clubface, toward the sky through impact.

These keys will allow you to pick the ball cleanly off the turf and hit a soft-landing shot that trickles toward the hole. When you hit down too sharply, dirt inevitably intervenes between the ball and clubface at impact. As a result, the ball flies much farther than normal. When you're trying to hit a delicate shot, you don't want to be factoring in the flyer element.